FOR
Oliver and Amber, Hannah, Robert, Niall, Andrew.

Main Street, Marceline, Mo.

For Walt Disney the
happy memories of a childhood in Marceline
remained with him always. When some
fifty years later, Walt added a main street to
Disneyland, it was Marceline that provided
the inspiration.

Walt Disney's
WORLD OF FANTASY

ADRIAN BAILEY

COMPILED AND DESIGNED BY JULIE & STEVE RIDGEWAY

New York EVEREST HOUSE *Publishers*

Published in the United States of America in 1982 by Everest House, 33 West 60 Street,
New York 10023 and simultaneously in Canada by Beaverbooks, Don Mills, Ontario by arrangement with
Dragon's World Ltd. Printed in Hong Kong
Library of Congress Cataloguing in Publication data:
Bailey, Adrian, 1928-
    Walt Disney's World of Fantasy
    1. animation (cinematography). 2. cinematography--
special effects. 3. Disney, Walt, 1901-1966. 1. title.
TR897.5.B26   791.43'75   82-1547
ISBN 0-89696-117-6   AACR2

CONTENTS

INTRODUCTION

THREE YEARS AFTER the debut of Mickey Mouse in *Steamboat Willie* in 1928, the magazine 'Vanity Fair' nominated Mickey's creator for their Hall of Fame, the first but by no means the least of Walter Elias Disney's 900 citations, 32 Academy Awards, 5 Emmys and 5 honorary degrees: Walt Disney was to become the most decorated man in movie history.

'Vanity Fair' was dedicated to a belief in the progress and promise of American life, which it chronicled with wit and sophistication, nominating newcomer Walter Disney:

> 'Because he is the creator of an immortal and irresistible hero of the animated cartoons – Mickey Mouse; because he inspired *Silly Symphonies*; and because, while still a young man, he has produced a new form of amusement – the synchronised and animated cartoon.'

To assess the true value of Walt Disney's unique contribution to entertainment and graphic art, which the British cartoonist David Low enthusiastically compared to that of Leonardo da Vinci, we must look objectively at the many influences that have shaped Disney's vision and his world of fantasy.

Certain elements of the fantasy, as some see it, contain the ingredients of sentimentality and violence.

It is true that Disney could be sentimental, as expressed in some of the sequences in Bambi, or in the relationship between baby Dumbo and his mother, scenes that deeply touched many audiences. It is, furthermore, impossible for the human mind to dwell for long upon fantasy devoid of violence – the two are inseparable.

Above all, Walt Disney was a great storyteller in the ancient tradition of the fairy tale – often as grim as Grimm, fanciful as Hans Andersen, fantastic as Lewis Carroll, sentimental as Charles Kingsley. The story was conveyed too with a remarkably accurate eye for detail and movement. The mouse dodging the raindrops in *Bambi* moves as only a mouse can move, not an anthropomorphic mouse like Mickey, but a scuttling rodent seeking shelter; the moment when Snow White, accompanied by all the woodland animals and birds, goes in search of the dwarfs' house is a masterly piece of animation by Hamilton Luske that drew applause from the audience when it was first shown in 1937. Disney had the magic touch, of which he was certainly aware: the Sorcerer in *Fantasia* is named 'Yensid' which, if held up to the Wicked Queen's mirror would read 'Disney'

It might seem reasonable to object to Walt Disney's claim that his films are aimed at adults as well as children, since so many of his plots are taken from the fantasy of fairy tales – *Mickey and the Beanstalk, Three Little Pigs, Cinderella, The Sleeping Beauty, Snow White*, drawn from what many would see as mankind's age of innocence. But were these stories devised for children? Cinderella is the tale of a (presumably) teenage princess who conquers adversity to marry a prince and live happily ever after, a rags-to-riches story that appeals on many levels, one of which is deeply subconscious and atavistic and the reason that the story has appeared in no fewer than 350 versions throughout the world. The stuff of dreams is powerfully attractive, and Disney exploited it to the full.

Essentially, Walt Disney was the right person in the right place at the right time, and it is unlikely that he could have become Walt Disney, the impresario of fantasy, 'The Twentieth Century Aesop', anywhere else but in Hollywood.

Some of his American critics may deplore his cultural contributions to the national heritage, but the fact remains that

Disney was totally American. Like Hoagy Carmichael and Will Rogers he was the product of Midwestern, homely virtues and its enviable optimism.

Above all Disney approved of the ethic of hard work; he also had the determination to succeed, and the vision of the pioneer.

ADRIAN BAILEY. HOLLYWOOD. CALIFORNIA
1981.

'You observe not only people but animals, draperies when the wind blows, waves in the sea, or smoke in a fire. There are a million things to observe and file away in your brain.'

The next stage in the animated cartoon awaited the professional or, to be more accurate, a professional approach, since the animated cartoon with a story line and satisfactory structure had yet to be born. The new medium would need an artist of exceptional skill and inventiveness, one with a sense of style and, of course, a sense of humour.

TEN THOUSAND DRAWINGS

Walt Disney promoted himself on his first letter-head.

IN 1906, JAMES STUART BLACKTON, a staff artist on the 'New York World' produced a film where he drew faces on black paper with chalk, which he called *Humorous Phases of Funny Faces*. The animation was done by progressive drawings, each one erased between camera takes – or more accurately, the part that was required to move was erased so that the next sequence of movement could be drawn, shot on a single frame of cine film, then erased. The film showed a man rolling his eyes and blowing smoke rings, a girl winking, a dog jumping through a hoop. It was great stuff, and the public flocked to watch Blackton's moving cartoon. He eventually became a film director and a millionaire, developing a cine camera and founding the Vitagraph Film Corporation – but his cartoons fell some way short of the excellence of those made by his successor, Winsor McCay.

McCay was the doyen of cartoonists, and his regular strip *Little Nemo in Slumberland* (perhaps influenced by *Alice in Wonderland)* was a remarkable fantasy world of dreams and magic.

Winsor McCay is often credited with being the inventor of the cartoon film, and certainly his famous *Gertie the Dinosaur* is a prominent landmark in the panorama of movie history. Like Disney, McCay recognised the importance of drawing and detail – he was widely held to be the greatest cartoonist of his day – and his animation drawings set very high standards for those animators who followed. As far as the audience was concerned, McCay's films of *Little Nemo* and *Gertie the Dinosaur*, which he combined with live-action sequences as part of a vaudeville act, were little short of miraculous. How did he do it? Wires, maybe? Then McCay informed his audience that *Gertie* was the result of ten thousand separate drawings, each one photographed on a single frame of film. The audience probably found the explanation impossible to comprehend, concluding that only an artist would be crazy enough to attempt it. Ten thousand drawings for three minutes of film?

Winsor McCay was a pioneer in the sense that he was treading unexplored ground. Labour saving and shortcut techniques, such as drawing on celluloid sheets or 'cels', patented by Earl Hurd in 1914, and Raoul Barre's 'slash system' which saved having to retrace the entire drawing for each movement, had yet to be invented.

ANIMALS AS HUMANS

The newspaper cartoonists and illustrators were not slow to recognise the possibilities of animation, which also provided an additional outlet for their

Art Department

regular work. If audiences chuckled over *Little Nemo*, they'd roll in the aisles over the antics of *Mutt and Jeff*.

Although cartoon characters had a ready following, the studios saw the need to create characters of their own. The most famous – indeed, internationally famous – cartoon of the 1920s was *Felix the Cat*, drawn by Otto Messmer for the Pat Sullivan Studio. *Felix* followed the successful strip cartoon *Krazy Kat and Ignatz Mouse*, a wild, intellectual fantasy cartoon, created by George Herriman. Ignatz was a philosopher. 'Oh, would that some kind magic ease the woe I feel' he sighs, sitting on the brick he regularly threw at the Kat. *Krazy Kat* and *Felix* set the trend for anthropomorphism in cartoon that reached its peak with *Mickey Mouse* in the 1930s and today's current obsession with Charles M. Schulz's *Snoopy*.

This book is no place to go into the psychology of anthropomorphism, why we invest human characteristics (we might not like what we find) but the formula is well-tried – novelists Stevenson, Kipling, Barrie and Kenneth Grahame all recognised the attraction in the fantasy of animals with human characteristics. 'We possess a kingdom of our own,' wrote Walt Disney, 'in which animals and even inanimate objects speak, think and act like human beings, but with far greater charm.' Disney had a rich source of animal magic in Carlo Collodi's *Pinocchio* and Felix Salten's *Bambi*.

Felix the Cat was a great character. He was, if you like, 'the thinking man's cat', pacing backwards and forwards, head bowed in thought, paws clasped behind his back. His influence on Disney's earlier cartoons appears as Julius the Cat in the *Alice* series.

In one of the first Felix cartoons, *Felix Trifles with Time*, he meets Father Time, who is persuaded to take Felix back to the Stone Age. Father Time winds back the hands of a large alarm clock, until the dial reads 'Stone Age', and Felix finds himself in a desolate, rocky landscape over which he is pursued by an assortment of prehistoric monsters, to the unlikely accompaniment of the tune 'Turkey in the Straw'. The film was later given a sound track. After many narrow escapes Felix is rescued by Father Time, and quits pre-history to take refuge in a twentieth century garbage can, so that the fade-out gag could then be emphasised, 'No more Stone Age for me—give me the garb-age...'

Left, Top: The art department of Kansas City Film Ad service in 1920, where Disney learned the rudiments of cartoon animation. Below: *Walt posing at his desk. He made cartoons and took part in live-action commercials for local theatres.*

Felix was launched in 1919, the year that the young Walt Disney started in Kansas City. If it were merely a matter of precedence the East Coast studios had the edge on Disney. They were experienced, they had the distribution, and above all had established the popularity of their creations with their audiences.

AN APTITUDE FOR DRAWING

In 1919 Disney was unknown, a tall, gangling teenage kid with a rural background to whom the familiar epithet 'greenhorn' might well apply. Yet in the next eight or nine years this raw recruit to the film industry would make more than eighty films, and achieve world wide fame with Mickey Mouse. Part of Disney's success was due to his remarkable tenacity and his skill as an innovator. But there was something else: Walt was a loner, and he was utterly ruthless in his aims, a quality not uncommon in artists. He roamed his own patch of territory, first in Kansas City, then in Hollywood, while his competitors drank from the same spring in New York. He admired and envied the work of the New York school, just as they would soon admire and envy him. One of the animators from Charles Mintz's studio later recalled, 'We were always trying to figure out why he was so successful, and we were usually wrong.'

Walt Disney was eighteen when he arrived in Kansas City. He had no professional experience, his

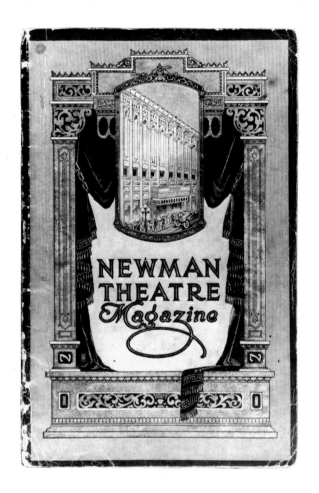

excursions into art had produced average results, although his first attempts were auspicious: family legend says that the young Walt covered the outside walls of his family home with sketches in tar. The American painter Thomas Hart Benton, who also grew up in Missouri, remembered the same attraction for large areas of white – he drew freight trains on the freshly papered walls of his parents' house. Both artists had big-screen concepts, for Benton eventually became a mural painter, and Disney a movie producer.

From early on Walt had shown an aptitude for cartoon drawings, and to perfect his technique he took lessons from professionals such as Carey Orr, famous political and editorial cartoonist of 'The Chicago Tribune', and had collected a gag file while attending performances of vaudeville and burlesque. What kind of gag? In one of Walt Disney's earliest films a cat is thrown down a flight of stairs, 'What's the matter – miss your step?' asks his companion. 'No,' says the cat, 'I hit 'em all.' He eventually built up a sufficiently impressive portfolio to secure himself a job with the art studio of an advertising agency, Pesmen-Rubin, who offered him fifty dollars a month, an attractive offer since young commercial artists worked for crusts of bread in order to gain experience and collect a portfolio of published drawings.

American advertising was then, as now, the voice

Left: *Cover design by the versatile Walt Disney, drawn in 1919 for the Newman Theatre, Kansas City.* Above: *Walt as cameraman. For the young cartoonist it was a short step from the drawing board to the movie camera.*

of commercial enterprise and progressive marketing. If this seems over-simplistic it is well to bear in mind that in Europe the mass production of consumer goods – especially automobiles – and the concept of a consumer market was unknown. Press advertising was mainly typographical and the poster was a by-product of fine art, exemplified by such artists as Lautrec, Mucha and William Nicholson.

In America the poster came into its own, with the expanding development of the automobile industry and, during the First World War, the propaganda poster. Illustration and poster design was taught in American schools, influenced by such notable designers as Maxfield Parrish, Robert Wildhack and J. C. Leyendecker. The leading magazines – 'McCalls', 'Vogue', 'Harpers', 'Vanity Fair' and the 'Saturday Evening Post' depended upon illustrations as the newspapers depended on the cartoon.

There was money, enthusiasm and there was hot competition in the still buoyant economy, and it gave great impetus to the graphic arts. The 'Saturday Evening Post' began to use a young and promising new talent – Norman Rockwell. Rockwell and Disney have much in common, aiming at an almost identical audience and sharing a similar response. Both men were great storytellers, and both shared a passionate dedication to detail, which Norman Rockwell acknowledged when he presented one of his paintings to Disney, with the inscription, 'to

Far left: *The Laugh-O-Gram studio in 1922. The poster advertises "Jack and the Beanstalk" and credits "Walt Disney", early establishing the Disney name. Above: Clip from the Laugh-O-Gram "Puss in Boots". Left: A title frame.*

Walt Disney, one of the really great artists, from an admirer.'

BITTEN BY THE BUG

In 1919 Walt Disney had some way to go before attaining this stature, but the Pesmen-Rubin studio gave him some commercial experience and enabled him to meet other talented artists and designers, one of whom was to greatly influence his future. Working at Pesmen-Rubin was a young artist of Dutch immigrant parents whose name wouldn't raise any eyebrows in Amsterdam, but cinemagoers in Kansas City responded to the credit 'Ubbe Iwwerks' with amusement – and they would also remember it. Of greater significance was the fact that Ubbe was a good draughtsman and a cartoonist of rare and natural talent; he and Walt Disney

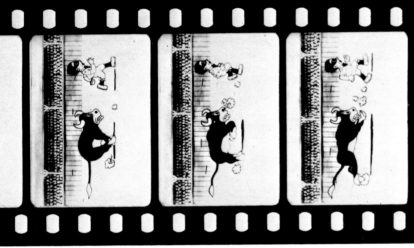

were destined for greater things than a career in a design studio. Their future, and the subsequent history of animation, was in the balance when Walt tipped the scales by answering an advertisement put out by a company making lantern slides.

Kansas City Film Ad Company produced crude but effective animated cartoons, made from paper cut-outs, which merely inspired Disney to seek a more effective method by using drawings. He studied Muybridge's photographic experiments in animal motion, which were the outcome of a bet made between two horse fanciers – 'Is there any moment when a galloping horse has all its feet off the ground?' The answer, by the way, is 'Yes, there is', and Muybridge went on to produce some fascinating freeze-action of ostriches, pigeons, and eventually humans in motion.

Left: *Laugh-O-Gram studio business card.* Above: *Figure from "Puss in Boots", one of six cartoons loosely based on traditional fairy tales. The cartoon company, formed in 1922 with animator Ub Iwerks, was Walt's second business venture.*

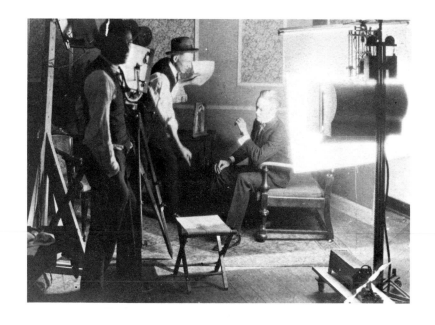

They were a great help to Disney, and so was a book on animation, the first of its kind, that had fortuitously just been published by E. G. Lutz in 1920 – 'Animated Cartoons', which described among other things how to ink cels, how to register paper by slotting it on metal pegs, and such tricks as the pinwheel effect of two figures fighting, which was used in several early Disney shorts. Eventually Disney was able to put the new techniques into practice – prints of these films exist and are historically interesting.

ALICE IN WONDERLAND

Walt Disney's independence and the progressive drive which marked his career now began to assert itself.

He quit Film Ad, and teamed up with Ubbe Iwwerks to produce a series of films which they called *Laugh-O-Grams*, a series of short cartoons, based – oh, so loosely – on several of Grimm's fairy tales. *The Four Musicians of Bremen* is far more entertaining than Grimm's original tale, a zany fantasy in which the 'musicians' – a cat, a cockerel, a dog and an ass are pursued across country by a swordfish! They fall down a chimney into a house full of German alpine troops then commence bombarding the house with cannonballs until it resembles an Emmenthal cheese. These early films are crammed with visual puns – the passage of time is

RODOLF'S REVENGE

Far left: *Disney as director on a live-action film "Martha", made for the Jenkins Music Co. Assisting Disney are staffers Adolph Kloepper and Ub Iwerks. The adjacent pictures are a title frame and a Laugh-O-Gram poster.* Left: *Walt Disney in Swope Park, Kansas City, 1922. With him are Max Maxwell, Rudolf Ising, Ub Iwerks, Hugh Harman and Bob Huffe.*

indicated by flying alarm clocks – and odd touches such as the army nurse who waves a Red Cross flag at a flying cannonball which develops a face that nods sympathetically, and swerves aside.

The films were successful, but the company's finances were shaky. Animated cartoons, however simple, were costly to make (between one and two thousand dollars for a seven-minute short), and Disney insisted on ploughing back the slender profits in order to perfect the product. In truth, Disney's films at this period were comparable to many of their more experienced competitors in New York, the centre of the industry. But to forge ahead he needed a gimmick. Once more Disney turned to the world of fairy tale and fantasy for inspiration. How

The first Alice cartoons, distributed by Margaret Winkler and made in Hollywood. Disney combined a live-action girl with cartoon figures and wrote to Winkler "...I assure you that I will make it a point to inject as many funny gags and comical situations into future productions as possible."

about 'Alice in Wonderland'? Why not take a live-action Alice, mused Disney, and have her appear in a cartoon wonderland? The live-action cartoon combination had been popular ever since Max Fleischer had started his *Out of the Inkwell* series, in which an animated Koko the Clown appears from

the cartoonist's pen or inkwell and performs in live-action surroundings. Walt decided to reverse the process with a live-action little girl, and chose a precocious six-year old called Virginia Davis who, in several respects, predated the later Shirley Temple.

Disney's first Alice film, *Alice's Wonderland*,

bankrupted the young film maker, and left him understandably depressed and disenchanted with Kansas City as a place of fulfilment. New York was the cartoonist's mecca but Disney, remember, was a loner and fiercely individual. Moreover, pioneers went west, not east, so Walt Disney, with forty dollars and a suitcase, caught the train for California's orange groves and the hills of Hollywood, to create a legendary career and an immortal mouse.

Disney admitted being 'bitten by the cinema bug at a time when you still called it cine', but Walt wasn't exactly seeking employment in Hollywood, although he had toyed with the idea of becoming a movie director. As it turned out his first studio was in the rear of a real estate office on Kingswell Avenue and here, in 1923, with his brother Roy as business partner, Walt began production of the *Alice Comedies* series.

He had managed to raise funds by getting a New York distributor, Margaret Winkler, to agree to financing an *Alice* series on the strength of his original Kansas City film, in which the shrewd distributor had spotted above-average promise. The fact that Disney had left the star of his films in Kansas City was resolved when her parents agreed to move to California, Walt having offered to pay Virginia Davis one hundred dollars a month. He also needed Ub Iwerks (who had shortened his name), and with some difficulty and a promise of one hundred and

sixty dollars a month, coerced Iwerks to come to Hollywood. The first *Alice* cartoons were rough-hewn, simple films, made by shooting Alice against a white background, then marrying the film to a print bearing the animated figures. This had the effect of making some of Alice's movements jerky, sacrificing the fluency of the live action for better quality animation. Also, the films had the disadvantage of being high-key, with intensely white backgrounds.

Nevertheless they contained many original sight gags in addition to those that were common property to all cartoonists and animators. Sight gags — humour that relied almost entirely on visual action — were vital to the cartoons of the silent era, as they were to the movies of Chaplin, Buster Keaton and Harold Lloyd. To get the spoken word across, animators often employed the cartoonist's balloon technique or the lettered titles interspersed between action sequences.

Action was the important feature, of course. Violence that preceded or led to the chase was the stock-in-trade of most animators, since they could then exaggerate movement — it was mainly for practical rather than psychological reasons that violent action featured regularly in silent movies, as

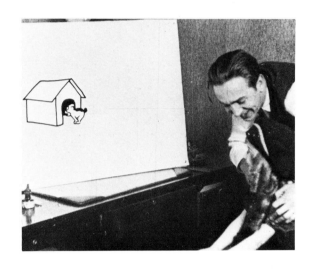

Left: *Alice was inspired by Max Fleischer's "Out of the Inkwell" series with an animated Koko the Clown in a live-action setting.*
Above: *Walt and "Alice" — Virginia Davis — in the studio. A still from "Alice's Wonderland".*

it had done for centuries in Punch and Judy shows. The violent interaction between two opposing characters can be as vital to comedy as it is to drama. The trend persists to this day, though the psychological element has somewhat taken command.

The first *Alice Comedy* film opens with a live-action sequence showing a young and dapper Walt, but minus moustache, demonstrating to Alice how cartoons are made. Cartoon animals then start to interact with the live-action background – the studio cat (cats are lucky mascots in film studios) is teased by an animated mouse who prods him with a sword. Alice then goes home to dream that she's in cartoonland, where she is pursued by a quartet of rather lumpy lions, who possess the rare talent among lions of being able to remove their dentures so as to sharpen their teeth with a file, a gag Disney repeated in the 1930 *Silly Symphony*, *Cannibal Capers*.

In all, Disney produced fifty-seven *Alice Comedies*, before they were phased out in favour of *Oswald the Lucky Rabbit*. He had personally made most of the animation drawings for the first six cartoons, before Ub Iwerks joined him from Kansas City. Iwerks's arrival meant that Disney could co-ordinate animation procedures, originate story plots and gags, and establish the role he was to play for the rest of his life – the organiser, the processor, and the final arbiter of all the studio produced.

Left: *A poster for "Alice in the Jungle"*, Above: *Disney dressed 1920s Hollywood style, outside the Hyperion studio. The little girl is the second Alice, Margie Gay, accompanied by cartoon characters.*

CAT AND MOUSE

Walt prepares the Disney Bros. Studio truck on Roy's wedding day.

THE ALICE SERIES WAS a useful proving ground for Disney; it also enabled the audience to acquaint themselves with the cartoon film as a medium, and to identify with the little girl, while enjoying her adventures in a fantasy world, although the concept had its limitations. The early *Alice* comedies show the influence of other studios and cartoon makers: in *Alice's Spooky Adventure* she shares the screen with a character that was to become her companion through many adventures, a cat named Julius who, like Pat Sullivan's Felix, can remove his tail and use it like a club. In *Alice Chops the Suey* there's a spoof on Max Fleischer's *Out of the Inkwell* series, when a black silhouette climbs out of an inkwell to be revealed as a live-action Alice.

Towards the end of the *Alice* series it became obvious that she lacked the comic personality of such competitors as *Felix* and *Krazy Kat.* It is very hard to balance a real person against animated characters so that both react satisfactorily together. Dick Van Dyke and Julie Andrews got away with it in *Mary Poppins*, but in the later *Alice* films the character of Julius the cat began to dominate and to assume more importance than Alice herself; the original star, Virginia, had since been replaced by Margie Gay.

Another problem was that the films had always

been financially unstable, and the series gradually ran out of steam. Part of the trouble arose from the fact that Margaret Winkler, Walt's New York distributor, had married and decided to retire. The business was taken over by her husband, Charles Mintz, whose subsequent relationship with Disney was less than cordial.

Walt could possibly have dropped Alice altogether, and concentrated on developing Julius, but there were too many cats around. Felix was being compared to Charlie Chaplin as a forceful comic character.

Krazy Kat was marginally less successful. Drawn by Bill Nolan and distributed by Mintz, Krazy had somewhat lost ground when compared to the original George Herriman newspaper cartoons. Krazy's off-beat humour and potent appeal to the subconscious of his readers was fine in print, but it didn't translate well to the movie screen. Nevertheless, cartoon animals were reaping profits at the box office. Universal Studios' boss Carl Laemmie wanted a piece of the action, and was looking around for a studio to create a new character. But what? A cat – a mouse? Laemmle didn't know, but finally plumped for a rabbit. 'Funny', mused an editorial writer of 'Film Daily', 'why nobody thought of a rabbit before.'

Charlie Mintz, who dealt with Universal, suggested that Walt Disney might be the person to

develop a rabbit figure. Disney made preliminary sketches and sent them via Mintz to Universal – the sketches were approved and Walt was invited – or perhaps commanded – to make a pilot film. Walt now had a rabbit, but it was without a name. Mintz, so the story goes, put several names into a hat, and drew out one bearing the name 'Oswald'. What neither Mintz nor Disney appreciated at the time was that Oswald was owned by Universal, the rabbit was Laemmle's idea and he established the copyright; this fact would be painfully revealed to both Mintz and Disney in the future.

In the four years that had passed since Disney arrived in Hollywood, Walt had found time to marry one of the studio's ink-and-paint girls, Lillian Bounds. (An ink-and-paint artist traces the pencilled sketches onto the 'cel', then applies the tone or colour.) The studio had expanded to include animators Rudolf Ising and Hugh Harman (who later joined forces to make the 'Harman-Ising' cartoons for MGM), Isadore 'Friz' Freleng, Rollin Hamilton and Walker Harman. The studio needed more space, and moved to premises in Hyperion Avenue, off Sunset Boulevard in the Silver Lake District – not exactly Hollywood, but near enough. Here they began to produce *Oswald* films – an average of two a month. The Hyperion studio had several advantages over its competitors – including a new product – *Oswald* – the trade magazine 'Film Daily'

Above: *Cartoon characters from the "Oswald" series.* Right: *The growth of the Hyperion studio from the original building seen in the small picture below to the expanded site, photographed in 1933.*

reporting that 'Oswald with his long ears has a chance for a lot of new comedy gags and makes the most of them,' also several of the best animators in the business, especially Ub Iwerks who was not only the most inventive, but the fastest animator of his day.

Disney had just completed the *Alice* series, and the studio was getting into its stride with *Oswald*, when an event occurred that was to alter the entire movie business forever. In October 1927, Warner's premiered Al Jolson in *The Jazz Singer*, the first sound movie, but the message would take two or three months to sink in, before the other studios, including Disney, awoke to the challenge.

Meanwhile, the experience which Walt had acquired producing the *Alice* series was proving invaluable in creating Oswald. Disney knew the im-

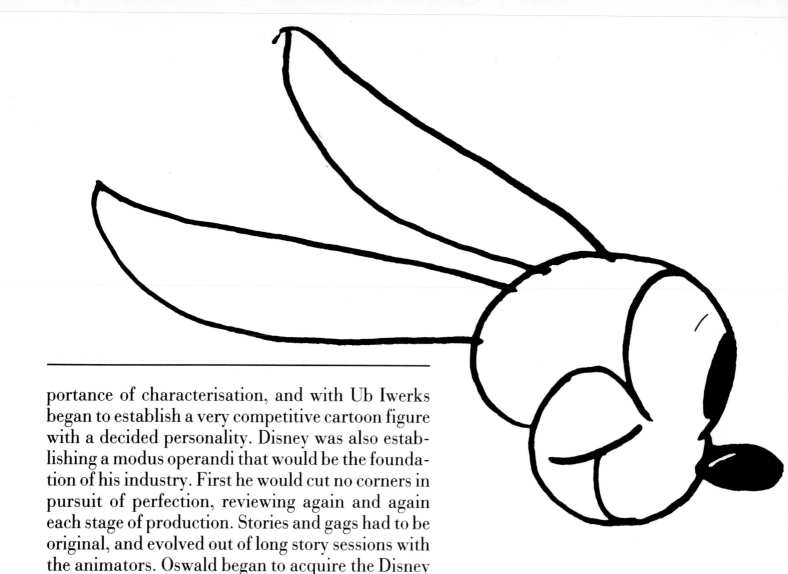

portance of characterisation, and with Ub Iwerks began to establish a very competitive cartoon figure with a decided personality. Disney was also establishing a modus operandi that would be the foundation of his industry. First he would cut no corners in pursuit of perfection, reviewing again and again each stage of production. Stories and gags had to be original, and evolved out of long story sessions with the animators. Oswald began to acquire the Disney image – he was appealing, flexible and inventive.

In the 1928 cartoon *Bright Lights* Oswald tries to sneak past a theatre doorkeeper, who smashes the rabbit with his fist. Oswald separates into several tiny replicas (as the brooms do in 'The Sorcerer's Apprentice' sequence in *Fantasia*) then reassembles. Oswald is pursued on stage where he hides in a 'box'. The box turns out to contain a tiger. Oswald screams and instantly shrinks so that he can slip out of the bars of the cage. So does the tiger! He chases Oswald and is joined by a trio of lions, and later the entire menagerie. As they rush from the theatre the building deflates like a pricked balloon.

BURLESQUE BOYS

With the *Oswald* series Disney was also establishing a future routine of spending more money than production costs could bear. Perfection paid off in terms of the finished product, and rival studios tried to find out if Disney had some sort of secret method.

—AND LAST BUT BY NO MEANS LEAST Oswald THE LUCKY RABBIT

The first choice of all cartoon comedies among thousands of wide-awake exhibitors

In one short season OSWALD has leaped to the top in popularity with millions of movie fans.

Twenty-six in the series—created by Walt Disney—Winkler Productions. Released thru UNIVERSAL.

In addition to the OSWALD Series you get these corking one-reelers produced by Universal.

13 HORACE IN HOLLYWOOD
starring ARTHUR LAKE

13 LAEMMLE NOVELTIES
{Something new under the sun}

WATCH the Universal Weekly for further important announcements on UNIVERSAL'S HEADLINERS for 1928-29

Said animator Paul Terry, who admitted to being more interested in quantity than in quality, 'Disney is the Tiffany's, and I am the Woolworths.'

In Leonard Maltin's excellent and comprehensive book, 'Of Mice and Magic' the author was told by animator Frank Thomas that Walt 'had the talent to draw out of guys what they didn't have'. Certainly Oswald was a true Disney product, and the prototype of Mickey Mouse. At first, Oswald went barefoot and wore only trousers with a single suspender strap. Later versions have him wearing the outfit that Mickey would inherit: large white boots, white gloves, short pants with two large buttons – Mickey is a slimmer Oswald, with rounded ears and a long, thin tail.

There seem to be faint echoes of other influences in the designs of Oswald and Mickey Mouse, a touch, perhaps, of the blackface minstrel from early burlesque. Unlike Goofy, Mickey is never a clown,

Oswald the Lucky Rabbit. Later he was given the oversize shoes and two button trousers that Mickey Mouse would acquire. Animated by Ub Iwerks and Isadore "Friz" Freleng, Oswald was a force to be reckoned with in the cartoon industry. New York animator Dick Huemer, seeing an Oswald cartoon on Broadway, was "considerably impressed and not a little jealous".

but his role as a figure of fun is established by elements that are traditional provokers of mirth. Laughs were guaranteed in the routine of burlesque comics by over-large shoes, the big nose, illfitting

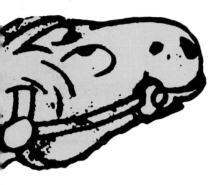

trousers with a single suspender.

The creation of Mickey Mouse, and his transition from the character of Oswald occurred when Charles Mintz made the mistake of thinking that he and Universal could do without Disney. The decision came about after Universal had reviewed the costs of the series. Other studios kept within their budgets — why couldn't this guy Disney do the same, instead of asking for more money?

The solution, decided Mintz, would be to sign up Disney's staff, and begin a fresh series of *Oswald* cartoons — minus Walt. To Disney's astonishment and dismay, all his animators quit to work for Mintz, all, that is, save for Ub Iwerks who was to defect later. Mintz offered a higher salary and perhaps the promise of an improved status, which effectively compensated the animators for any feelings of disloyalty to Disney.

Charles Mintz had unwittingly done Walt a great favour: Disney swore that never again would he lose control over his interests. More than anything else this incident established Walt Disney's future – it made him totally independent, it showed him the value of marketing his products, and emphasising the Disney name and Disney image.

NOTHING TO LOSE

Walt Disney liked to relate the story of how the idea for Mickey Mouse occurred to him during a train

Left: *From a dealer advertisement for an Oswald cartoon of 1927, distributed by Universal. This one was called "Empty Socks".*

journey, basing his character on that of a real mouse, one of several that inhabited Walt's Kansas City studio, but it is equally likely that Mickey was created on Ub Iwerks drawing board under Walt's direction and advice, and was a metamorphosis of Oswald.

Originally the mouse was to be named 'Mortimer', but whatever his origins, Mickey's prolonged birth caused as much anxiety to Disney as to any

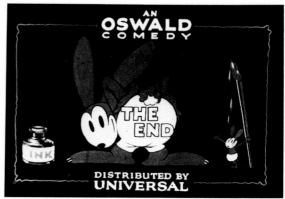

parent. Once having decided to launch a new character, Walt and Ub worked flat out to get the first film off the ground – an apt simile since it was to be based on the current national adulation of Charles Lindbergh who had just made aviation history. In his own quiet way Iwerks now made animation history by producing 700 drawings for their new film *Plane Crazy* in a single day – an astonishing average of one drawing per minute! Mickey's second

Oswald and his successor. Mickey was born when Disney was forced to lose Oswald to the distributor Charles Mintz. To replace their rabbit Disney and Iwerks created a mouse, and Mickey's first film "Plane Crazy" was completed in a record two weeks!

cartoon, *Gallopin' Gaucho*, quickly followed and, with his two films in the can, Disney set out for New York to find a distributor.

There now occurred another of those strokes of fate that helped shape Disney's future. The success of *The Jazz Singer* had shaken the movie industry out of its complacency. Studio bosses argued for and against the new medium, actors were fearful — especially Chaplin, who resisted sound to the end.

Kevin Brownlow, in his movie history 'The Parade's Gone By...' describes the arrival of sound as a brutal transplanting instead of a gentle grafting:

> 'the cinema was ripped out of the silent era by the roots, and transplanted into new soil — richer but unfamiliar. Unable to adjust to the new conditions, some of the roots withered and died, and much strength was lost!'

Disney however, trying to establish a new character in a new series, had nothing to lose. He was quick to realise that here was a golden opportunity to exploit the new medium by adding sound to animation. Disney was halfway through the third Mickey cartoon, *Steamboat Willie*, inspired by the title of a recent Buster Keaton success *Steamboat Bill Jnr.*, and halted production to accommodate sound. He would make the world's first sound cartoon, but the question was — how do you marry the sound effects to the action? The simple answer was — use a metronome. One of Disney's animators, Wilfred Jackson, possessed a certain musical talent

and suggested that rhythm and sound effects could be matched to the frames of animation. Since the film ran through the cine camera at a speed of twenty-four frames per second, those that emphasised a particular action — a falling brick, a drumstick hitting the drum — could be related to the accent or beat in the music or the essential sound effect say every eight frames or multiples of eight.

Disney and the animators rigged up a rough demonstration for themselves which, said Disney later, 'was terrible, but it was wonderful! And it was something new!' and from Iwerks, 'I've never been so thrilled in my life. Nothing since has equalled it.'

TURKEY IN THE STRAW

The New York distributors were less enthusiastic, because it was an innovation, and the sound of music was still a hot topic of controversy, especially in the field of cartoons. Walt Disney had considerable trouble (and no little expense) to get his film shown; inefficient or costly sound systems forced him into a deal with a rogue promoter, Pat Powers, who at least deserves the credit for supporting Disney and providing equipment for several of his first sound movies, even though he grabbed a lion's share of the profits.

In all events the film, *Steamboat Willie*, was a great success with the audience, and it scooped good press reviews, including the 'New York Times', who

Drawings from a character model sheet showing typical Mickey poses and actions.

WALT DISNEY STUDIO
MICKEY MOUSE
SOUND CARTOONS
2719 HYPERION HOLLYWOOD

BURTON F. GILLETT   OLYMPIA 2911

thought the film an ingenious piece of work, and welcomed 'a new cartoon character henceforth to be known as Mickey Mouse'. By today's standards, *Steamboat Willie* is almost prehistoric in content and execution, yet its farmyard humour has some strongly conveyed sight gags, and Iwerks's animation gives an excellent rendering of movement and weight.

The musical score, by Carl Stalling, includes the inevitable 'Turkey in the Straw' which Mickey and his consort Minnie use to improvise on the steamboat's cargo. Mickey, taking a couple of spoons from the ship's galley, plays the tune on a washboard, pots and pans, the ship's cat, a goose, some piglets, a cow's udder (which reaped the biggest laugh from the audience) and finally uses the cow's teeth as a xylophone. The fact that the animals undergo alarming indignities is one that is generally overlooked, for cartoon characters appear never to suffer lasting harm in the service of humour – just think of Tom and Jerry – it has become an intrinsic part of the fantasy.

Steamboat Willie may not have been a great cartoon, but it was as good as any of its contemporaries, and moreover it possessed the magic of sound. Another point in its favour was this – the early talkies were often badly made, they were dull, slow in action and the sound synchronisation was poor. They fell a long way short of the beauty and charm

"It was terrible, but it was wonderful!" Mickey Mouse in "Steamboat Willie", 1928. Al Jolson's "Jazz Singer" encouraged Walt to add sound to his latest film.

Scene # 27.

C.U. Mickey drumming on bucket and
utensils.....Goose in crate showing
at left of scene....Little Kitten
walks across scene ' MEOW'ING ' as
it walks across.....Mickey sees it
and puts his foot on its head and
pulls its tail in time to music....
and cat lets out yells in time to
last half of Verse.....He sees goose,
lets cat go and picks up goose....
puts its body under his arm and
pumps it in and out as he head and
neck back and forth like TROMBONE--
in time to verse......
SOUND EFFECTS....Squeaky cat sounds,
....WA - WA- WA- effect with sliding
trombone as he plays on GOOSE....

Scene # 29.

Medium shot of little girl turning
goats tail like crank....and music
of ' Turkey in the Straw ' comes
out his mouth like hand organ....

As she cranks che does crazy clog
dance........

Scene # 30.

C.U. of Mickey drumming on bucket
Old cows head sticking in left side
of scene....she is chewing in time
to music.....she reaches over and
licks Mickeys face with her long
tongue....then smiles (shows teeth)
Mickey sees teeth....opens her mouth
wide and hammers on her teeth like
Playing Xylophone....plays in time to
music....runs up and down scale, etc.
    Just as he is about to finish two
large feet(the Captains) walk into
right side of scene and stop....Mickey
finishes piece with 'Ta-da-de-da-da-...
on cows horns....pulls out her tongue
and strums 'Dum - Dum...' on it...and
turns around to girl with smile....He
sees feet...looks upslowly...when he
sees its Captain he acts surprised...

of the silent films, but cartoon belonged to neither category. As the critic Gilbert Seldes observed, 'The great satisfaction in the first animated cartoons was that they used sound properly—the sound was as unreal as the action...' The cartoons made the awkward transition from the silent era into sight and sound far more successfully than the first talkies, and the audience responded with applause, indeed, by 1930 Mickey was established as cinema's most popular cartoon character.

Walt Disney knew what he was doing, and later, when someone referred to the success of *Steamboat Willie*, Disney mused, 'Well, I guess I'd finally sprung the old Mickey Mousetrap.' It was to be the first of many.

THE DUCK AND THE GOOF

The *Mickey Mouse* films were remarkable in their variety, their changes of mood and atmosphere, but Mickey, engaging though he was, could not go it alone. Like many comedians he needed a foil and a back-up team, and thus the other Disney characters gradually made their appearances: Horace Horsecollar and Clarabelle Cow in *The Plow Boy* in 1929; Pluto in *The Chain Gang*, 1930, (but was not called Pluto until *The Moose Hunt* of 1931); Goofy took his bow in the 1932 film *Mickey's Revue*, with gag-writer Pinto Colvig, onetime circus clown, supplying Goofy's 'Aw Shucks' gurgle. Goofy or 'The Goof' as he is affectionately known at Disney's was brought to life by Art Babbitt. 'Goofy,' said Babbitt, 'was the kind of character that thought very hard and very long about everything he did. And then he did it wrong!'

Donald Duck first appeared in *The Wise Little Hen* in 1934, about a hen who tries to enlist the aid of neighbours to harvest her corn. The pig next door feigns tummy-ache, so does the owner of a barge – Donald – moored on the river. Only when the hen sits down to a feast of buttered corn and hot corn bread, from which Donald and the pig are excluded, do they realise their folly. Donald's endearing, pugnacious character is absent from this gentle film, and his saga only blossoms to the full in *The Orphan's Benefit.*

Left: *Stills from "Steamboat Willie". The rustic, barnyard humour was typical of the period – and the audiences loved it.*

"OKAY—OKAY—

NEXT AMATEUR
IS ___

"QUACK-QUACK"

Story sketch from the 1937 cartoon "Mickey's Amateurs" featuring Donald Duck and Goofy, and the voices of Walt Disney (Mickey) Clarence Nash (Donald) and Pinto Colvig (Goofy).

By the early 1930s Mickey Mouse had become a world-wide cult figure to a degree that was hard to explain. With his hopeful, high-pitched voice (Disney's own – he played Mickey for most of Mickey's career) the Mouse exemplified the optimism, determination and the true grit possessed by Disney himself, and the pair were closely identified.

Mickey Mouse was a moral hero, but a moralist with a sense of fun, and above all a symbol of a carefree philosophy which the audience shared. It should also be remembered that Mickey was cleverly promoted, and with a success that has only recently been equalled by Schulz's Snoopy. Mickey was featured on cups, plates, spoons and serviettes,

on watches, alarm clocks, stationery, cookie tins and, during the Second World War, on the noses of B17s that flew over Germany.

Mickey's spirit of fun greatly appealed to the audience of the times, and the films were crammed with action. In *The Whoopee Party* of 1932, directed by Wilfred Jackson, Mickey and Minnie hold a party in their home, and amongst the guests is Goofy. The guests dance, sedately at first, to the tune of 'Sweet Rosie O'Grady', then the tempo gradually warms up. Minnie, at the piano, starts to belt out a faster rhythm, and the guests improvise on anything that comes to hand. As the dancing becomes more and more frenetic, even the furniture, lamps, kitchen utensils, and the piano become animated and join in. Finally as the entire house threatens to burst at the seams, the police arrive: they join in of course, for was not this the great era of Makin' Whoopee, of Paul Whiteman the King of Jazz, and the Golddiggers of Broadway?

In direct contrast, Mickey appeared in a 1933 Gothic cartoon called *The Mad Doctor*, in which the Disney animators allowed their fantasy for the macabre a considerable licence. A cloaked and hooded figure steals Pluto away in the night, carrying him – howling – to a Frankensteinesque castle lit by a Dracula moon. Once in the castle, the abductor reveals himself as a mad (and decidedly Slavic) 'doctor' who clamps Pluto to a dungeon wall

Left: *The Mickey Mouse years at the Hyperion studio, and the expanding Disney staff. Animators and story men bore Walt's own character in mind when working on a Mickey cartoon Mickey was said to reflect many aspects of Disney, and Walt always did Mickey's voice-over. The pictures opposite show Walt at the drawing board, also animator Norman Ferguson, using a mirror to capture a facial expression.*

to await 'experiments'. Pluto's howls bring Mickey hurrying to the rescue, and after a series of incidents in which Mickey is pursued by skeletons, (skeleton vampire bats, a fearsome skeleton spider, and even the cuckoo in the cuckoo-clock is a skeleton) the doctor captures Mickey and straps him to an op-

Above: *Story sketches from "Thru the Mirror", 1936, a cartoon based on Carroll's classic "Alice Through the Looking Glass". Right: Poster for "Mickey's Good Deed", 1932.*

erating table. In an episode that Poe might have created, a circular saw begins to descend from the ceiling, and is just about to snare into Mickey's trouser buttons when... Mickey wakes up from his nightmare. His yells bring Pluto, plus kennel, bounding through the window, and Mickey hugs the dog with relief.

KEEP IT CUTE

With Mickey Mouse on his way to fame and fortune, Disney's musical director, Carl Stalling, made a further contribution to the repertoire by suggesting a series of films based upon musical themes, using melodies from the classics as a key for the visuals.

Although Walt himself could hardly be described as musical, 'I've a tin ear' he once remarked, he acknowledged the value of music in cartoons and furthermore he wanted to encourage Stalling's talents. Another reason, Disney explained later, was due to the fact that he didn't want to be stuck with the mouse'.

The *Silly Symphonies*, as the films were to be called, acted as a foil to the humour of Mickey. For one thing, they did not rely on a star character, but were in a sense far more flexible in that they exploited the endless possibilities of the animated cartoon. For another, they were ahead of their time in sophistication, their approach to fantasy, and their appeal to the more reflective moods of the audience. Yes, they

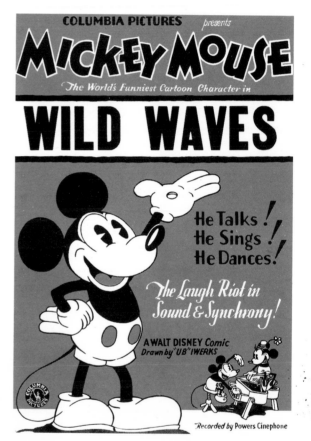

"Wild Waves", the 15th Mickey Mouse cartoon, was made in 1929, when posters continued to stress the arrival of sound. Max Fleischer had actually made synchronized sound cartoons as early as 1925, with sound pioneer Dr. Lee De Forest, but they were not commercially viable.

sought to amuse, but also to touch other chords in the viewer's responses.

The *Silly Symphonies* were witty, fanciful and inventive, but they also contained a generous measure of the whimsy that Disney insisted on injecting into all his films. Animator Don MacPherson, who worked in the Disney studios on *The Sleeping Beauty* feature during the 1950s, recalled that Disney had a reminder pinned over every animator's desk, that bore the message, 'Keep it cute.'

Donald Duck strikes a typical fighting pose in this story sketch.

GIFT OF THE GAG

THE FIRST SILLY SYMPHONY, made in 1929, *The Skeleton Dance*, revealed in every way the anatomy of the concept. The scene opens in a graveyard at night. Silhouetted against a full moon is an owl, perched on a branch, while below two scrawny black cats pull each other's noses. A skeleton appears, having risen from one of the tombs. The cats flee and the skeleton, hunched on a gravestone, suddenly launches itself at the camera, in what remains today an unnerving moment. Other skeletons then join in a graveyard frolic, one playing on another's vertebrae, like a xylophone to 'The Hall of the Mountain King' from Grieg's 'Peer Gynt'. This same tune was used by Fritz Lang in his unforgettable film *M* based on a true story of a Dusseldorf child murderer, and it is interesting to speculate whether Lang, who made the film in 1932, saw Disney's *Skeleton Dance*, and remembered the haunting quality of the music.

The animation by Ub Iwerks, who practically viewed the film as his personal property, is precise, and the dance of the four skeletons to a sort of fluid, houri routine is compelling to watch.

The Disney animators loved comparing bones and dentures to the resonant, staccato sound of the xylophone – Mickey started it in *Steamboat Willie* and it is used again in *Cannibal Capers*, a 1930

Silly Symphony where skulls serve as castanets, to a melody from Bizet's 'Carmen'. With the production now divided between the Mickey Mouse series and the *Silly Symphonies*, Walt Disney hired more animators, including Ben Sharpsteen, who would later win recognition for his work on *Snow White*, and Bert Gillett, who worked on many of the *Symphonies*, and was responsible for directing Disney's first Academy Award winners, *Flowers and Trees*, and *Three Little Pigs*.

Gillett was 'poached' by the Van Beuren studio in 1934 – but that was the name of the game, animators were usually hired and fired several times throughout their careers, and offers of more rewarding salaries was only part of the reason for this apparent fickleness. Animators were, after all, artists. They possessed that 'artistic temperament' which usually meant that they merely wanted to be admired for their talent and creativity.

Although Ub Iwerks was loyal to Disney during Walt's conflict with Charlie Mintz, the seeds of discontent were being sown. Aside from Walt himself, Ub Iwerks was the major architect of the Disney image and the legend; Iwerks virtually created *Mickey Mouse* and did many of the early cartoons singlehanded. He was prominently credited for his work, and Disney acknowledged his contribution, yet Disney's was the name the public knew.

Both men had started out on an equal footing in

Kansas City, but it was Walt who had the ideas, the gift of the gag, and eventually the public image. In short, Walt Disney was the boss and Ub Iwerks was the employee. When Pat Powers offered Iwerks the chance of going it alone, and to set him up in his own studio, Ub agreed. He left Disney, and persuaded Carl Stalling to join him, and began to develop his own cartoon character Flip the Frog.

Iwerks' association with Disney had lasted eleven

79

years, and Disney was reportedly stunned by Ub's departure. Iwerks signed off with Disney on *Arctic Antics*, the eleventh of the *Silly Symphonies*, and Bert Gillett more or less stepped into Iwerks' shoes. *Winter* is a typical cartoon of this period. Set to the 'Skater's Waltz' of Johann strauss, the film opens with a snow scene, and bear cubs asleep outside their

"The Skeleton Dance" animated by Ub Iwerks and released in 1929, was the first of a new series of "Silly Symphonies". It remains a classic of the early sound cartoon.

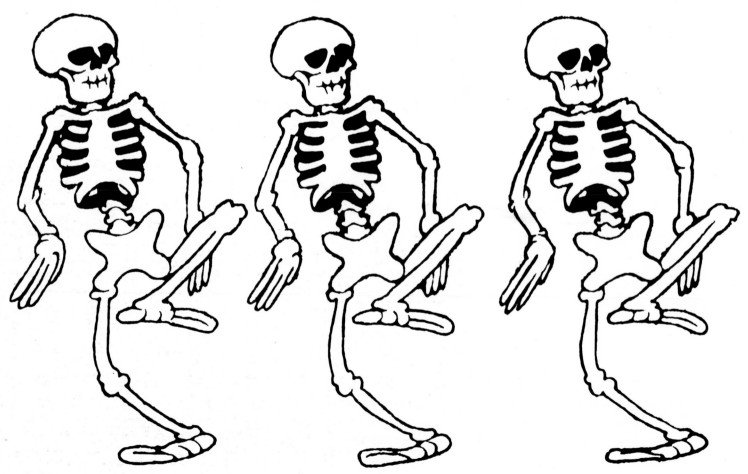

Story sketches and a background painting and cels for the 1937 Silly Symphony "The Woodland Cafe", directed by Wilfred Jackson. That same year Jackson also directed the award-winning 1937 cartoon "The Old Mill", a Disney masterpiece that has never been surpassed.

cave. Groups of animals come to frolic in the snow and skate on the ice – racoons, rabbits, foxes, bear cubs, reindeer, and a ram that skates on his curved horns. A gentle film, with such sight gags as a bear that plays chimes on hanging icicles, a swimming moose that employs his antlers as paddles, and a groundhog that is chased across the snow by his own shadow. By later standards this is simple and primitive stuff, but it was good animation experience, and each cartoon film improved on its predecessor.

GIVE THE PUBLIC WHAT IT WANTS

Disney was not merely well in touch with the times, he was ahead of them, at least in terms of the animated cartoon. At the beginning of the 1930s the

Cels and story sketches from "The Woodland Cafe", and a portrait of a famous character the Disney staff affectionately called "The Goof".

studio had introduced new techniques and methods
of production. Walt encouraged the staff to contri-

bute gags, sketches, story ideas, anything that was grist for the mill. He paid a bonus for ideas, although the 'encouragement' was more in the nature of a directive from High Command:

PLEASE DRAW UP ALL SUGGESTIONS AND GAGS READY FOR COLLECTION BY THURSDAY, 9 A.M. WALT.'

The course of each story, emphasised at certain points by actions and gags, was plotted on a story-board, a system unique to the Disney studio and generally credited to storyman Webb Smith, the first to use a visual sequence system. Sketches of the action were pinned in sequence on a large board, which enabled Disney and his animators to see the essence of the cartoon at a glance, where the weaknesses lay, and where a different approach might be

"The Orphan's Benefit", 1934. It established an irascible but lovable duck named Donald as a character in his own right, although Donald had first appeared in an earlier cartoon, "The Wise Little Hen". "The Orphan's Benefit" was remade in 1941.

taken. It gave the Disney films a firm structure and storyline that rival cartoons usually lacked. The system is still used by film and television producers, and in publishing where a picture book can be developed by the 'flap plan'.

Disney pioneered many of the techniques of animation that became standard practise in other studios. Animators would first make character sketches, followed by drawings that would establish the key positions in the action of a figure or object. The various degrees of movement between one key pose and another (bear in mind that each frame of film is represented by one drawing) were done by the assistant animators, called 'in-betweeners', and other artists who tidied up each drawing – 'cleanup men' – as it came off the drawing board. Walt also introduced pencil tests, a film comprising a series of

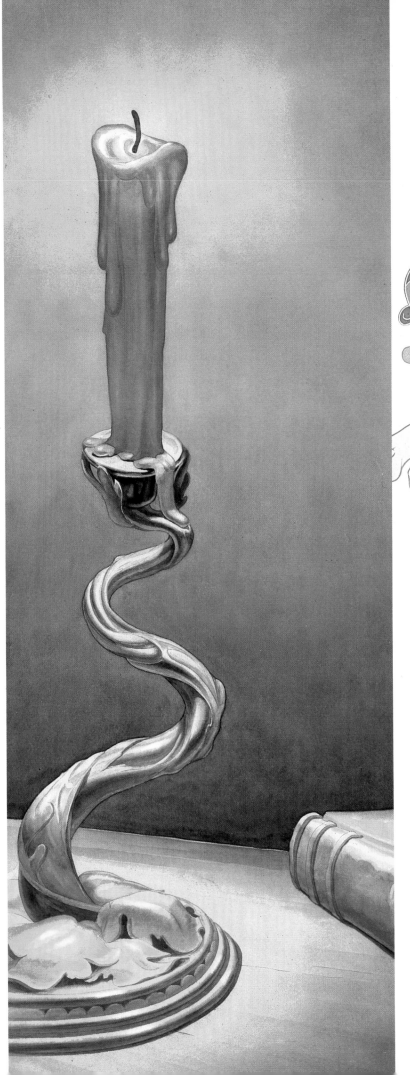

Left: *Background painting from "Lonesome Ghosts" with Mickey below, being stalked by a rather overweight "ghost" in a derby. Directed by Bert Gillett, the cartoon was released in 1937. Gillett also directed "The Moth and the Flame". A detail from a background painting for the cartoon is shown on the near left.*

pencil drawings to give a reasonably clear idea of how a finished sequence might look. Finished drawings were then transferred to cels by 'inkers' and the colour applied by 'painters'.

It was inevitable that the next technical advance would be the introduction of colour, and equally inevitable that Disney would be the first to use it. He had meanwhile severed his relations with Pat Powers and Cinephone to join Columbia. This was to be a shortlived affair when Disney's production costs rose to around 15,000 dollars per picture, which Columbia considered to be an unreasonably high figure, especially for a cartoon.

But Disney believed that no expense should be spared in the effort to please his audience. In 1948 he wrote:

'Nowhere else does any entrepreneur make such an effort to give the public what it wants...'

Columbia Pictures may have been shortsighted – and short of money – but a group of independent

Panorama of a street scene from "The Country Cousin," a Silly Symphony that won the 1936 Academy Award. The cartoon was directed by David Hand, and contains the famous sequence where the country mouse, let loose on a table in a metropolis of hams and cheeses – including a Gruyere like the Empire State – gets drunk on champagne. He sees his friend the town mouse in triplicate, and whose image remains in triplicate to us, the audience, even when the country mouse closes his eyes.

producers who called themselves United Artists saw
the potential in Walt Disney, and made him an offer
he could hardly refuse – a 15,000 dollar advance on
each film, guaranteed financing and exclusive distribution of his cartoons.

Although the American people were weathering
the worst economic crisis in their country's history,
the future looked promising: Franklin Delano
Roosevelt was the new President, and he had prom-
ised Americans, a 'new deal' of economic reform to
combat the depression; prohibition was repealed,
and the Golddiggers of Broadway were humming
their optimistic hit, 'We're in the money'.

FIRST IN COLOUR

Even with the security of United Artists' contract,
Disney was not exactly in the money, but he was
encouraged to take the next step and make a colour
cartoon – against the advice of everyone in the studio, particularly Roy Disney, who thought the outcome would be financially disastrous. Predictably,

Walt wasn't to be budged, and equally predictably he used his powers of persuasion to win his brother around. Walt was right, of course – colour was the next stage in the progress of motion pictures, even though the experiment was so far untried.

There had been many attempts at producing satisfactory colour movies. G. A. Smith's additive process, known as 'Kinemacolor' projected a two-colour image which suffered from colour fringing, especially with fast-moving subjects. Cartoons adapted far more readily to the colour process, and one of Ub Iwerks' early 'Flip the Frog' cartoons, *Fiddlesticks*, is in black, red, and green.

The Technicolor Organization, formed in 1915, had perfected a two-colour dye transfer process and in 1933 produced a three-colour subtractive process that could photograph the image through a tri-colour filter on to a single strip of film. It was not

only perfect for cartoons, but as far as Disney was concerned, it came along at the right moment.

Technicolor granted Disney a two-year exclusive deal, and Disney stopped production on his latest *Silly Symphony, Flowers and Trees* and scrapped the black and white footage to remake it in colour. Nobody was surprised when they ran into technical problems. For one thing, the paint wouldn't adhere to the cels, and colours faded to pastel hues under the hot lights. After weeks of experiment the artists found permanent powder colours which, when mixed with gum arabic, did not chip or flake; Walt Disney was about to make history with the first full colour cartoon, and it premiered at Grauman's Chinese Theatre in Hollywood, on July 30, 1932.

Flowers and Trees is a wonderful essay in fantasy, colour and advanced technique, albeit with a rather quaint story line: the film opens on a sylvan

Far left, top: *Captain Katt opposite one of the "Three Blind Mouseketeers".* Left: *Sam Armstrong studying a background painting for "The Old Mill".* Above: *Storyman Harry Reeves acts out a scene from "Good Scouts".*

93

glade at dawn. The principal characters are a young male tree with a shock of palm-leaf hair; an elegant female tree with a coiffure of verdant foliage and a face reminiscent of Jean Harlow; and a malignant, denuded, gnarled old tree. The young trees are in love, and as dawn breaks they yawn and stretch, flowers yawn and stretch, mushrooms spring up out of the soil. The gnarled tree wakes, yawns, and bats fly out of his mouth. Trees and flowers dance to a bird chorus, the female tree shedding a few delicate leaves as she moves.

The gnarled, grey tree now tries to abduct the female, and here there's a fragment of accompanying music that is particularly apt — Schubert's setting of the poem (by Goethe) about an evil wood spirit, the 'Erlkonig', one of the most menacing of

AN → MICE LAND IN SCENE PAN

Schubert's songs.

The tree is rebuffed and in revenge sets fire to the forest; a green serpent appears in his mouth while flames dance through the forest to the tune – rather strangely – of 'The Campbells are Coming'. The gnarled tree, caught in the fire, burns to ashes, and the flames are arrested only when birds puncture holes in the clouds with their beaks to release rain. Order is restored to a motif from Rossini's overture 'William Tell' and the film ends as the lover trees are married to the Mendelssohn 'Wedding March'.

The artists' treatment of the flames as relentless, dancing figures with almost human characteristics is beautifully done, and Disney was to repeat the idea several times, especially in *Elmer Elephant* and *The Moth and the Flame*.

Alexander Dumas would have loved it – a story sketch from the 1932 Silly Symphony "Three Blind Mouseketeers", showing the high standard of artwork and attention to detail in the background drawings.

Scene I

first pig
building
straw house.

Scene II

Second pig
building
house of Sticks

Scene III

Third pig
building
house of brick

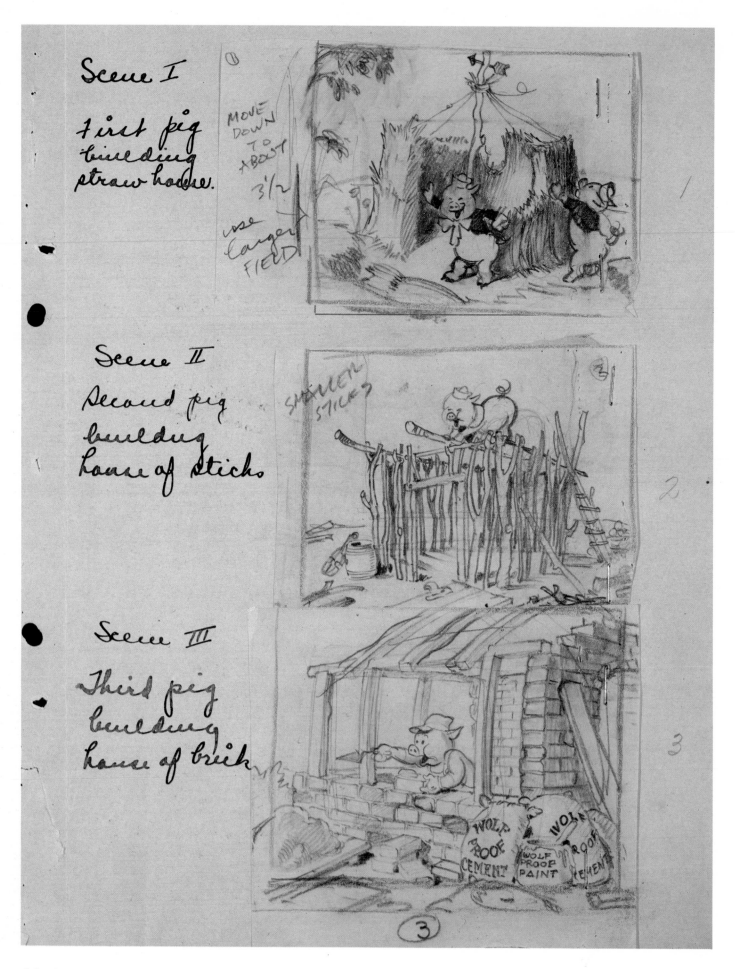

CARICATURE OF LIFE

Flowers and Trees not only won popular acclaim, but also Walt Disney's first Academy Award. From now on all *Silly Symphonies*, with the exception of *Bugs in Love*, would be in colour. The second Academy Award followed a year later with *Three Little Pigs* which introduced, for the first time in a cartoon, a theme song that incidentally became a hit: 'Who's Afraid of the Big Bad Wolf?' The song was written by Disney staffers Frank Churchill, Ted Sears and Pinto Colvig, while the wolf was devised and animated by Norman Ferguson.

The wolf is magnificent. Black and shaggy with prominent fangs and baggy trousers held by a single strap, he hefts a carpet bag. (His creator, animator Norman Ferguson was renowned for his ability to turn out forty feet of animation film a day.) The pigs by contrast to the wolf are pink and silly – at least, two of them are. The third pig embodies the principles of self-sufficiency and common sense. He wears a working man's overalls, a peaked cap, and wields a cunning trowel to build his house of bricks. Resourceful, he protects his companions from the hungry wolf, and in this cautionary tale movie philosophers have seen the common man projecting his fears into the figure of the wolf – a symbol of economic depression – and vanquishing him. It is as good an advertisement for a building society as any I know. The fantasy certainly fulfilled the Disney credo:

Left: *"Three Little Pigs", and its theme song "Who's Afraid of the Big Bad Wolf?" won world-wide acclaim and an Academy Award for Disney in 1934. Two years later the pigs returned in "Three Little Wolves"*, (above).

'The first duty of a cartoon is to caricature life, to make fantasies of things we think of today...'

Three Little Pigs was a wild success, although costs were higher, and this latest Disney epic may remain the most popular short cartoon ever made. Apart from the sociological conclusions mentioned above, the reason for its remarkable popularity was perhaps due to the film's quality: here was a cartoon of a familiar folktale, brilliantly characterised, and presented with a high degree of no-expense-spared

Above: *"Three Little Pigs"*. Right: *"The line that made him famous was not 'To be or not to be' but 'Wanna fight?' " (Donald Duck described by Gerald Burtnett in the Los Angeles Times). Overleaf: Mickey wields the conductor's baton in story sketches for "The Band Concert", the first Technicolor Mickey Mouse cartoon, 1935.*

professionalism. On the other hand the *Mickey Mouse* films, inventive though they were, remained in black and white, so that Mickey was obliged to wait until 1935 before he could boast a scarlet coat as the conductor of *The Band Concert* in a full Technicolor cartoon.

The concert begins with the overture to Rossini's 'William Tell' interrupted by the antics of a relentless Donald Duck, who insists upon playing 'Turkey in the Straw' on a tin whistle. A furious Mickey breaks the whistle in two, but Donald has an endless supply. The conflict is partly resolved by a whirlwind that comes sweeping across the prairie, sending Donald, Mickey and the players in a crazy spiral of colour and dissonance. The cartoon ends on the notes of 'Turkey in the Straw' – a triumph of Country and Western over Art, and Donald's squawk, originated by radio actor Clarence Nash, was given full range of expression.

The years between *Three Little Pigs* in 1933 and *Bambi* in 1942 became the Golden Era of the animated cartoon – at least for Walt Disney. Walt was now the acknowledged master or, as Hollywood nicknamed him, 'The Mousetro.'

If success went to Walt Disney's head, it certainly didn't show. The most likely effect would have been a cautious effort to avoid complacency and to take a hard look into the future. It is possible that Walt had nursed the idea of a full-length feature car-

Top: *Background painting for "Nifty Nineties"*. Left: *A cel from the 1935 Silly Symphony "Cock O' The Walk"*. Right: *Technician photographing rough animation sketches.*

toon – no, it wasn't to be a cartoon, but an animated film, a real movie – since the success of *Flowers and Trees*, and was preparing himself for the task. He also realised that an expansion programme was vital to the survival of the studio; the profit on a short animated cartoon barely covered the production costs, and Disney was a big spender – profits, even those with the slimmest margins, were invariably ploughed back in order to perfect the quality of forthcoming films.

The animated cartoon was no longer the poor relation of the feature movie, but was now demanding equal rights. Recognising this important advance, Walt Disney was encouraged to make the obvious comparison and ask himself the obvious question: 'Why not make an animated feature?' Why not? Not only was the idea revolutionary, but it is unlike-

ly that anyone else would have dared to take on
such a formidable task, or would be convinced of its
eventual success – imagine the number of individual drawings needed to make a full-length feature! And what about the cost? Had Walt weighed
up the pros and cons he might have decided to stick
to the cartoon short – but Disney was not that cautious. He had to make the first full-colour, full-
length cartoon film. He would call it *Snow White
and the Seven Dwarfs* – others were to know it as
'Disney's Folly'.

WHISTLE WHILE YOU WORK

WALT DISNEY APPROACHED the challenge of creating *Snow White and the Seven Dwarfs* with as much preparation as a general might plan a battle. He began by hiring Don Graham, an art teacher from the Chouinard Art School in Los Angeles as a permanent staff member.

Graham had helped Disney to form the Disney Art School in the Hyperion Studios, on a part-time basis, back in 1932, to help animators improve their technique.

A documentary film on the work of the Disney studios, made later, after the release of *Snow White* and in the interest of public relations, stated that:

> 'animation is the hardest art job in the world. It's also one of the highest paid. Good animators are rare, for their work requires flawless draughtsmanship combined with vivid, creative imagination.

In further pursuit of flawless draughtsmanship, Don Graham held day and evening classes, assisted by other art teachers, and with seasoned animators as guest lecturers. Reviewing the sketches made of settings, backgrounds and separate objects made during this period, one is struck by both the influence of commercial art and illustration of the Nor-

"Time" heralded the 1937 release of "Snow White and the Seven Dwarfs" with a cover story.

man Rockwell genre, and also by the influence of the fine arts. Elements of Art Nouveau and Art Deco, the Symbolists and Cubists, and of such American contemporary painters as Edward Hopper, Marsden Hartley and Joseph Stella, and of a particular American 'Broadway' art, exemplified in the routines of Busby Berkeley.

By 1934 Walt and his writers were holding regular story sessions for *Snow White*, and the studio had expanded to include additional story and gag writers, eighty-five animators and assistant animators, inkers and painters, an orchestra, and several departments of technicians. Also, new techniques were being developed, encouraged by the atmosphere of exploration. Filming animation sketches or pencil tests, and projecting them as 'rushes' so that the guts of the story could be swiftly assessed, had been in operation since the early *Mickey* cartoons. The films were viewed in cramped projection theatres which animators had dubbed 'sweatboxes', either because they lacked air-conditioning, or because of the critical presence of Walt at the viewing sessions – or both.

Another innovation of the period was the Leica reel which combined the pencil test and story sketches with the soundtrack to give a more accurate definition of the progress. The cartoons of the mid-thirties were a proving ground for techniques and stories, in preparation for the features to come,

Far left and below: *"Snow White and The Seven Dwarfs"*, *Walt Disney's first full-length feature, and certainly the most famous animated film of all time. Since its premiere during the Christmas week of 1937, it is estimated to have grossed almost 50 million dollars. Adriana Caselotti (left) the voice of Snow White.*

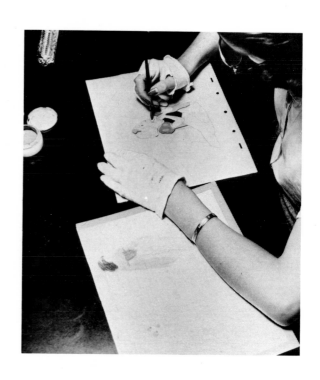

and many were to be reviewed in retrospect as classics of their time.

The *Silly Symphonies* continued to provide a flexible and important testing ground for techniques, gags and ideas. Two of these shorts, made within a year of each other – *The Country Cousin* and *The Old Mill* – are among the finest cartoons Walt Disney ever produced, and a fitting prelude to *Snow White*.

Surveying the history of the Disney studio during these years, one may be inclined to overlook the fact that while *Snow White* was being made, full production of the regular quota of short films had to continue. Top directors and animators such as Ben Sharpsteen, Art Babbitt, David Hand and Wilfred

Jackson not only played a major role overseeing and directing the production of the feature film, but worked on cartoons at the same time: David Hand and Art Babbitt on the Academy Award-winning *The Country Cousin*, and Wilfred Jackson on *The Old Mill* which also won an Oscar.

ESSENTIALLY GERMAN

Given the financial pressures and the tremendous amount of work involved (during the five years that *Snow White* was in production, animators made more than five million drawings and sketches, using five hundred miles of paper!) Walt Disney was besieged by problems and must have felt very lonely at times, even though it was his nature to go it alone.

Left: *The Ink and Paint Department makes its own special opaque colours from powdered pigment and gum arabic. The gouache is carefully painted on to the cels to fill in the line drawing.* Above: *Action is brilliantly conveyed in this animation sketch of Dopey, the most popular of the Seven Dwarfs.*

Snow White was an undeniable gamble, and to cope with the additional work, Disney called Don Graham and asked him to find three hundred extra artists, as if artists were as common to California as fruit pickers. By 1936 the ranks of the Disney staff had increased to over a thousand, and Disney was pressing for more talent for his Story Department:

'We must have good stories – we must have them well worked out – we must have people in there who can not only think up ideas but who can carry them through...'

Although good stories are the life blood of the cartoon maker, Disney knew that action and humour could become stifled where there was too much plot:

'Even in our first animated feature, *Snow White*, the original Grimm Brothers' version had to be considerably cut, though it was novel length and our picture was to last over an hour. Without cutting, there would not have been room for our sort of fantasy, our sense of humour, and the creation of our personages.'

So how much did Walt Disney's idea of fantasy differ from or distort the original? Well, there's brevity in both Disney and in Grimm. Disney minimises plot to give more elbow room for gags and action. Similarly the Grimms wasted no time on detail – the faster the action unfolded, the better.

Disney drew much of his material from the folk stories of all nations, and so did the Grimms: in a literary essay on *Snow White*, author Anthony

Can you name them? Sneezy, Bashful, Sleepy, Happy, Grumpy and Doc. Dopey, on the previous page, hasn't quite caught up.... Left, below: *Two of the forest creatures. Animation sketch of a rabbit and a chipmunk. What is a chipmunk doing in Ruritanian fairyland?* Overleaf: *Background painting and cel of the Queen who has transformed herself into an old hag.*

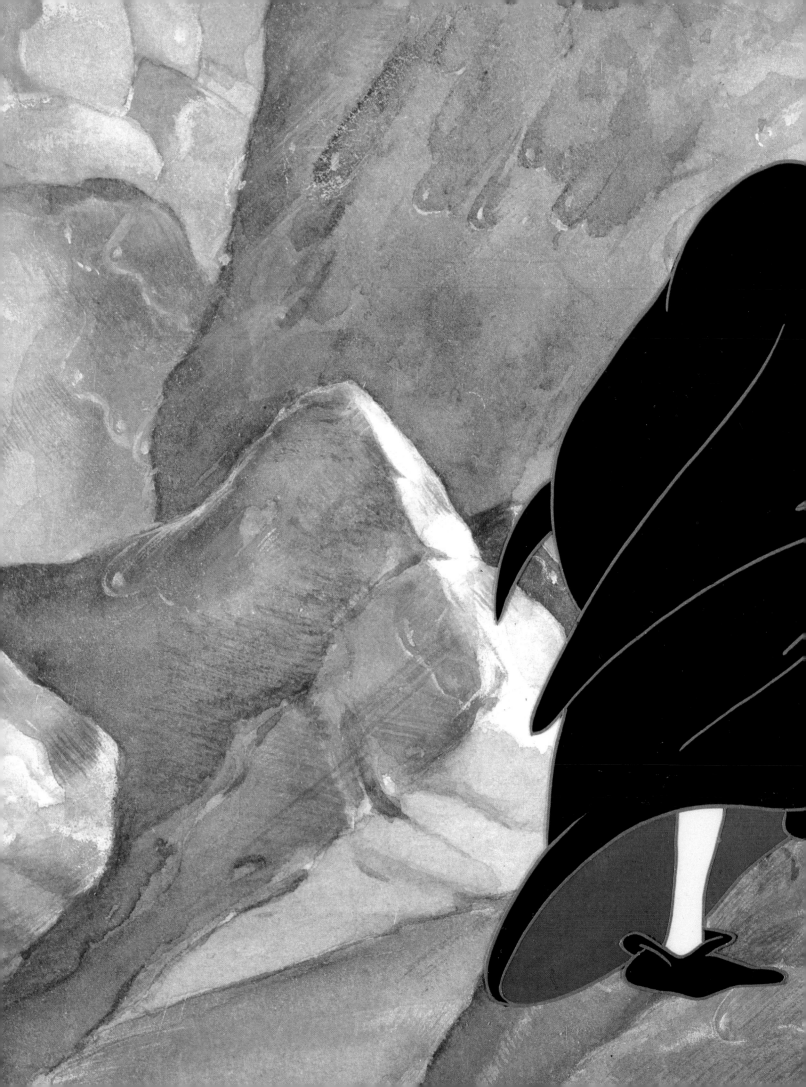

"Disney's Folly" Makes History

A Grimm fairy tale comes to life as something new under the sun .. Hollywood laughs at Hollywood, with music

Liberty - Feb. 12, 1938

By BEVERLY HILLS

★ ★ ★ ★ SNOW WHITE AND THE SEVEN DWARFS

Based on the fairy tale by the Brothers Grimm. Produced by Walt Disney for release by RKO-Radio Pictures. Running time, 82 minutes.*

THIS is Walt Disney's dream come true. For years he has hoped to make a feature-length film, a wholly animated production without human actors.

Snow White has a rare and elusive charm. It is a lovely translation of the old fairy tale created by Jakob Ludwig Grimm and Wilhelm Karl Grimm—the fantasy of the beautiful little princess who flees her wicked stepmother and comes to dwell in the depths of the forest with the seven dwarfs who labor by day in a jewel mine.

But the stepmother consults her magic mirror, summons all her black wiles, and sets out to kill the little princess.

Like all Germanic folk tales, Snow White has its vein of cruelty. It has fearsome things reaching out of the forest darkness to terrorize the fleeing Snow White; it has its horrible witch with her lust for blood. But the fable also has its beauty, its humor, its tenderness.

The birds, the squirrels, the forest hares, the fawns, all the shy folk of the woodland, do their best to help Snow White. Here the film achieves a lyric loveliness impossible to any-

*Recommended for children.

READING TIME ● 8 MINUTES 7 SECONDS

4 STARS—EXTRAORDINARY
3 STARS—EXCELLENT   2 STARS—GOOD
1 STAR—POOR   0 STAR—VERY POOR

thing of flesh and blood. Too, the fantasy, unbelievable as it may seem, possesses its tense and moving moments.

The dwarfs are individual and delightfully characterized, quaint little beings of fantasy.

Snow White is something brand-new under the Hollywood sun.

VITAL STATISTICS: Story's been left much as the Grimm Bros.—Jakob Ludwig & Wilhelm Karl—conceived it late in the 19th century. Chief differences: Animals and birds have been given human characteristics, dwarfs have been named Sleepy, Sneezy, Grumpy, Happy, Bashful, Dopey, and Doc and characterized sharply. Squatty, by the way, is a ringer for Dopey but wears a beard. Grimm Bros. won undying fame but few riches. . . Snow White's been 3 years in the making, tying with Chaplin's Modern Times for the longevity production record. Hollywood called it Disney's Folly. At world premiere, however, all Hollywood paid $5.50 a ticket, cheered Disney, speculators got $50 a seat. . . Disney artists are known as Disney's hands, work for from $19 a week to about $250 tops. . . None of the offstage voices in Snow White get credit, are sworn by contract to secrecy as to their identity, ride around in comfortable cars nevertheless. . . Walter Elias Disney is a 1-goal-handicap polo player, loves his 2 children to distraction, is happily and once married, he's

of Chicago birth and Missouri farm upbreeding. Studied drawing at Chicago night schools, was turned down for ill health when he applied as a postman in Chicago, went home, put on make-up and got the job. Spent two years driving a Red Cross war ambulance in France. His first art job was drawing farmyard animals for a Kansas City ad agency. While working nights over a drawing board a fat mouse ran out, made friends with him, got named Mortimer Mouse, later became Mickey Mouse after quite a struggle to crash world of animation.

★ ★ ★ HOLLYWOOD HOTEL

THE PLAYERS: Dick Powell, Rosemary Lane, Lola Lane, Ted Healy, Hugh Herbert, Johnnie Davis, Glenda Farrell, Alan Mowbray, Louella Parsons, Frances Langford, Mabel Todd, Ken Niles, Jerry Cooper, Allyn Joslyn, Duane Thompson, Edgar Kennedy, Grant Mitchell, Curt Bois, Fritz Feld, Eddie Acuff, Perc Westmore, Sarah Edwards, Clinton Rosemond, Wally Maher, William Davidson, Libby Taylor, Georgia Cooper, Paul Irving, Joe Romantini, Raymond Paige, Benny Goodman. Screen play by Jerry Wald, Maurice Leo, and Richard Macauley from a story by Mr. Wald and Mr. Leo. Directed by Busby Berkeley. Produced by Warner Brothers. Running time, 95 minutes.*

BUILT around Louella Parsons' well known radio hour, this is entertaining—and far too long.

The action centers around the imaginary Orchid Room of the equally fabulous Hollywood Hotel and shows a broadcast wherein the jobless would-be movie actor Ronnie Bowers (otherwise Dick Powell) goes on in an emergency and makes a great hit. The picture, too, delves into the secrets of picture making (if there are any secrets left) and laughs heartily at Hollywood.

Miss Parsons is completely herself

*Recommended for children.

Snow White and her forest friends, as they appear in Walt Disney's success.

Burgess, tells us that the first edition of Grimm's *Kinder und Hausmarchen* was written in honest dialect:

> 'with no High German sophistication. It was a vision of good old innocent Germany. What nobody saw was that it was not Germany or any other land, no matter how odd: it was all lands and all people...The stories are in various forms of German peasant language, and they contain German properties, like sausages and cheeses and beer, but there is nothing about them that we can call echt deutsch, "essentially German".'

NO GAGS IN GRIMM

Disney's *Snow White and the Seven Dwarfs* chooses to emphasise a powerful element of Teutonic folksiness, especially in the alpine architecture of the

PHOTOPLAYS

RADIO CITY MUSIC HALL
Showplace of the Nation   Rockefeller Center

"IF YOU MISS IT YOU'LL BE MISSING THE TEN BEST PICTURES OF 1938."
Frank S. Nugent, N. Y. Times

"Seldom has a picture been more hopefully anticipated. Seldom has one so completely fulfilled all its promises . . . a picture no one, be he five or fifty, can afford to miss."
Eileen Creelman, Sun

"One of the wonders of the modern cinema . . . the gayest, merriest, most imaginative film that has come out of Hollywood in years. There can be only one word for it—a word so much misused—'masterpiece'."
William Boehnel, World-Telegram

"Ranks with the greatest motion pictures of all time . . . a dramatic and moving work which will delight adults as much or more than children and will demand being seen time and again."
Howard Barnes, Herald Tribune

"Sheer delight . . . a motion picture miracle . . . there has never been a motion picture like it."
Rose Pelswick, Journal

"The entire audience seemed to fall under the magic spell and applauded with great enthusiasm . . . greeting each broadside of comedy with hearty guffaws."
Kate Cameron, Daily News

"Great—it will cast a spell over adults as well as over the young—for it has excitement, drama, wit, artistry and a most potent magic. Everyone must see it."
Bland Johaneson, Mirror

WALT DISNEY'S
SNOW WHITE
AND THE SEVEN DWARFS
A Full Length Feature in Multiplane Technicolor • An RKO-Radio Release

MARCH OF TIME · January Edition

ON THE GREAT STAGE:

"THE MAGAZINE RACK" the fourth annual edition of the Music Hall's colorful topical revue presenting in song and dance an interpretation of the leading international periodicals, including "Life," "Punch," "Sphere," "L'Illustration," and "Etude," produced by Russell Markert, settings by Nat Karson, featuring Viola Philo, Whitey and Ed Ford, Monroe and Grant, Helen Beebe, with the Glee Club, Corps de Ballet and Rockettes. Symphony Orchestra direction of Erno Rapee playing overture from Faust.

Doors Open Today and Tuesday 11:00 A. M.
Picture at 11:30, 2:05, 5:04, 7:57, 10:29 • Stage Show at 1:17, 3:51, 6:50, 9:25
FIRST MEZZANINE SEATS MAY BE RESERVED · TEL. COL. 5-6535

The press were sceptical, but the film produced ecstatic reviews. In Hollywood, "Beverly Hills" gave Snow White a four-star rating.

HIS FIRST FULL LENGTH FEATURE PRODUCTION

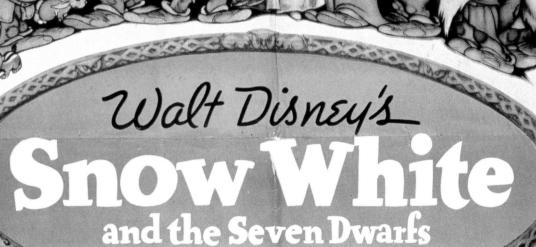

Walt Disney's
Snow White
and the Seven Dwarfs
in the Marvelous
MULTIPLANE TECHNICOLOR

©WDP

Distributed by RKO Radio Pictures, Inc.

dwarfs' cottage, with its rustic interior of sturdy oak beams, and carefully observed details such as jager horns and biersteins. Similarities between Disney and the Grimm Brothers are inclined to diversify when faced with the question of audience: who are the beneficiaries of these ancient moral tales – the children? 'Yes', said the Grimms, and called their stories 'Childrens' Tales'.

'No', said Disney:

'we make it our business to see to it our subjects appeal to children and adults as well, and at the same time we try to introduce action which will keep the children constantly amused, even if the subject occasionally goes over their heads. Our animated films must appeal to adults, since they constitute the major part of our audience.'

There are no 'gags' in Grimm, but the tales are sure to evoke nightmares, and dwell on brutality. Some critics thought Walt Disney's version of *Snow White* too frightening, especially for the children but Anthony Burgess points out that it was mild stuff compared to the original in which the Queen doesn't fall off a precipice. Instead, she is invited to the Prince's wedding, where at Snow White's command, she is forced to dance in red-hot shoes, until she drops dead. Not at all 'Disneyesque' says Burgess. 'It is, for want of a better term, decidedly grim.'

Yet Disney was not unaware of the importance of

All Hollywood turned up for the "Snow White" premiere. It was a supreme moment for Walt Disney and his wife Lilly (top picture).

drama, the balance of humour and menace, which Disney thought 'should strike when people are most happy'. Character was gradually defined as the planning progressed: the Queen was originally portrayed by Disney story men as a 'vain, batty, comedy type'. Then as 'high collar, stately, beautiful', and finally as a 'cold, tiger-woman type'.

Scenes subsequently deleted include one where the Queen has the Prince hanging in chains in preparation for drowning. Another where the huntsman, who had deceived the Queen, is dragged away by Nubian torturers, and a dungeon scene with dancing skeletons. Instead of the poisoned apple there was at first a poisoned comb (as in the Grimm version), but Snow White recovers. The magic mirror informs the Queen of Snow White's survival, the Queen flies into a rage and smashes the mirror to pieces, but the mirror reassembles itself, mocking the Queen and prophesying her doom.

By contrast, the characterisation of the dwarfs was a vital, comic element which Disney exploited to the full, the personality of each dwarf being painstakingly constructed during dozens of story conferences, until the dwarfs were almost a part of the Disney staff. Doc has a typical walk, and Walt described:

> 'Happy has a waddle, he's a little fat guy. Grumpy has that intent, matter-of-fact movement. Dopey is stumbling and tripping. I saw that a certain feeling was

Above: *Jiminy Cricket, Pinocchio's alter ego and the voice of his conscience. Jiminy, animated by Ward Kimball, featured but briefly in the original story, but Disney's Jiminy is a major figure.*

Left: *Geppetto's workshop, one of the background paintings reproduced here and on the following pages, that shows the unprecedented lavishness and detail typical of these early Disney masterpieces.*

needed that they had gone over the path so many times they knew every rock to avoid, like pack mules.'

SWEATBOX SESSIONS

From the point of audience reaction, and Disney made constant reference to the audience in these story conferences, the two principal dwarfs were Dopey and Grumpy. Dopey was a combination of 'Harry Langdon, Stan Laurel, Buster Keaton and Harpo Marx', while Grumpy was 'a pugnacious old sourpuss – the pessimist'. Dopey, like Harpo Marx, 'Don't talk none – he never tried', explains Doc.

Right from the early days of planning the animators and technicians were confronted by special problems: because of the immense amount of detail that went into every scene of *Snow White*, animation drawings had to be bigger than usual, which meant that each stage of processing had to be rescaled to adapt to the new format. In addition, Walt

Disney threw in extra problems that arose, almost daily, in his pursuit of perfection, re-assessing and correcting each development of production.

In a 'sweatbox' session over the question of colour, Disney told his animators:

> 'Inside the dwarfs' house I see a very rich effect obtained by throwing the distance in shadows and subduing a lot of background colours – not throwing them up in the face of the audience ... I think we are trying to achieve something different here ... we have to strive for a certain depth and realism.'

Depth and realism were problems inherent in cartoon making. It is difficult to obtain an illusion of depth and aerial perspective – when your camera tracks in for a close-up shot of a drawing, everything remains on the same scale, there's no difference in depth between the foreground and the background.

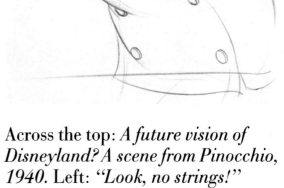

Across the top: *A future vision of Disneyland? A scene from Pinocchio, 1940.* Left: *"Look, no strings!"* Above: *The Coachman, who transforms boys into donkeys.*

Both Disney and Iwerks tackled this problem independently, and both came up with the same solution (although Disney's was more advanced) — the multiplane camera. Imagine a series of, say, four or

Far left: *Walt Disney with animator's reference model of Pinocchio the puppet, and cels from the film – Jiminy asleep in the scroll of a violin, and the two villains Gideon the Cat and J. Worthington Foulfellow, the Fox.* Left: *Pinocchio looks bewildered as he checks his script and the storyboard.*

five identical rectangular frames, each holding a painted pane of glass, positioned in the form of a long box, with spaces in between to create depth. Each pane (or glass plate) has a painted aspect of a scene or animated figures set up in a series of planes, rather like a toy theatre with stage sets. The panes are rigged to move in any direction on the lateral plane, the camera is likewise capable of infinite adjustment. The composite scene is then photographed by the camera, mounted at the end of the 'box'.

Left: *One of storyman Gustav Tenggren's studies for "Pinocchio".* Right: *Walt studies the story and Dickie Jones records the voice of Pinocchio.*

Cine camera lenses have an extended depth of field, so that foreground and background remain in focus, and this helps reduce problems of focussing, an additional problem being that of illumination — as few as four levels in the multiplane camera reduce the light by as much as 56 per cent. Shooting a scene in depth, with glass backgrounds on different planes moving in opposite directions with precise timing for a single exposure, is a highly complex procedure.

The camera was tried out, with great success, in *The Old Mill*; in the opening sequence the eye of the viewer is taken 'through' the landscape, past gently waving reeds, past meadows of grazing cows, across the mill stream to the mill itself. 'Just a poetic thing' said Disney, but in terms of technical innovation coupled with atmosphere, the film has never been surpassed. The camera was employed to a limited extent in *Snow White*, but the exploratory probing technique created wonderful scenes in *Pinocchio*.

When the completed footage of *Snow White* was reviewed by Disney in 1937, he decided that some sequences had to be scrapped, in order to cut down running time and achieve better balance. Thus an extended sequence of the dwarfs eating soup ended on the cutting room floor — expensive but necessary. As the preview deadline of December 1 approached, a worried director, David Hand, complained that animators were 'sitting on' some 1,500 feet of rough pencil tests, which they couldn't bear to release until they were perfectly satisfied, even though Walt himself was 'tearing his heart out okaying film which he would like to see better'. The film was completed in time.

EDUCATION IN FANTASY

To avert a possible nervous breakdown, Disney had taken a two months' vacation to Europe in 1935, but the fact that the press and the film industry gave a gloomy prediction for *Snow White* – 'Disney's Folly' they called it – only made Disney the more determined. Finally, *Snow White and the Seven Dwarfs* was premiered at the Carthay Circle Theatre in Los Angeles on December 21, 1937.

From the moment that the audience rose to its feet and cheered, the film was established as a movie classic on which generations of children were to be raised – an education in fantasy and whimsy that continues today.

On its release, the film generated an enchantment that was helped, to no small degree, by the music for *Snow White* is in effect a *musical*. The tunes are skilfully woven into the fabric of the plot, in the manner which Disney had achieved with *Three Little Pigs*, and subsequently pursued through *Pinocchio, Dumbo, Bambi*, and the astonishingly successful *Mary Poppins*.

Snow White is reputed to have cost one and a half

Pinocchio was released in 1940, but in spite of the huge budget of over two and a half million dollars, and some of the finest art and animation sequences ever produced, the picture was not a great success. The technique was dazzling, but the story lacked romance.

million dollars, and grossed over eight and a half million at the box office. It also won him a special Academy Award, presented by Shirley Temple, of a full-size Oscar and seven little ones.

PURE GOLD

PINOCCHIO WAS WRITTEN by an Italian author and educational reformer, Carlo Lorenzini, who published it under the name of Carlo Collodi, in 1883. It is in the tradition of the Commedia Dell' Arte, whose character Pulcinella was the original Punch, and in Russia is celebrated in the story of Petrushka. Ancient puppet tales, in common with folk stories, contain a rich vein of humour mixed with violence and morality. It is no exaggeration to say that the tales reflected many aspects of everyday peasant life, with Punch and Judy also acting out the eternal war of the sexes.

The puppets are in human form and they are invested with human foibles, vices and charms and, being controlled by automatic agency, are not responsible for their actions — and there is licence for almost boundless human fantasy.

Collodi's story tells of a puppet, Pinocchio, who is wilful, mischievous and provocative. His adventures are a series of predicaments in which his life is constantly threatened. Pinocchio wants to become a boy, and can reach this status only by showing sympathy and goodness. The story of Pinocchio is in effect that of mankind — we are all at the mercy of a greater power, and may reach salvation through love and the appreciation of moral principles.

Pinocchio is pursued by assassins, hanged by the

The hapless Mickey Mouse as "The Sorcerer's Apprentice" is tormented by brooms in a sequence from "Fantasia".

neck, suffers to have his feet burned off, is caught in a steel trap, nearly fried alive and is transformed into a donkey. In the film, Pinocchio merely gets the tip of his finger burnt – and cannot feel it.

As with *Snow White*, Disney felt obliged to alter the action and development of the story to make the character Pinocchio more appealing – Collodi's puppet is often thoughtless, deceitful and cruel, probably because the author needed a central figure whose provocative temperament evoked a powerful response from the supporting cast, which included Geppetto his 'father', the Fox and the Cat, plus a host of other characters.

Disney's Pinocchio lacks the charm of *Snow White*, and has none of the composite humour of the dwarfs, he is, in fact, an automaton. Faced with this dilemma, the Disney artists and storymen gave the leading role to the cricket, Jiminy Cricket, who introduces, right from the beginning, a source of humour. 'Phew!' says Jiminy, when the fairy brings the puppet to life, 'What they can do these days.'

In the original story, Pinocchio flattens the moralising cricket against the wall with a mallet right at the outset, the cricket only appears twice in the remainder of the tale – as a ghost, and later on the final pages.

Disney softens the character of the fiery Geppetto, and invests the Fire Eater (Stromboli) with more evil than Collodi visualised. Stromboli, who can

bend steel washers with his teeth, is a masterful piece of animation and characterisation by Bill Tytla. When Stromboli rages at Pinocchio, he makes hurried asides in Italian, which somehow underlines his menace, then locks the puppet in a birdcage, hanging from the roof of Stromboli's caravan. In the background, if you look carefully, you will see other puppets suspended from the roof, and as the caravan moves, the puppets also move with an undulating, rocking motion.

Animation can create actions much larger than life, and by emphasis make these actions even more convincing. When Geppetto jerks Pinocchio's strings, the lifeless puppet spins, leaps, falls down, and eventually collapses in a pile of wooden limbs.

Disney's *Pinocchio* is a film with a powerful atmosphere that is at times almost surreal, and in this respect takes its cue from the fantasy of the original. While *Fantasia* may be remembered for its innovation and audacity, *Snow White* for its charm and whimsy, *Pinocchio* will remain, in the years to come, as the supreme example of the art of the animated cartoon.

Fantasia is a collection of animated sequences inspired by pieces of music from the classical repertoire and remains Walt Disney's most controversial film. The London 'Times' in a retrospective review, said that *Fantasia* was a 'remarkably daring experiment that deserves to be remembered for its

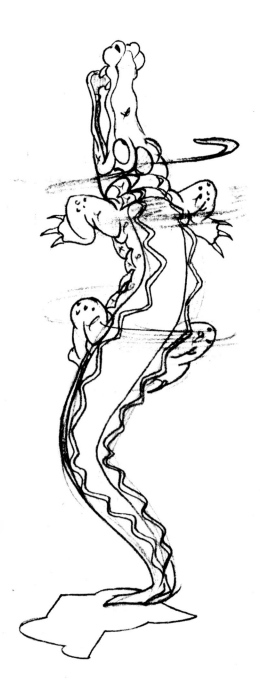

Preliminary paint sketches for the "Nutcracker Suite" from Fantasia. The alligator is an animation drawing for "The Dance of the Hours". Overleaf: Pastel sketches for the Centaurettes, and for Bacchus, from Beethoven's Pastoral Symphony.

successes rather than its failures'. Which would depend on your musical inclinations and tastes.

At a first glance the selection of pieces may seem

arbitrary, but it was based on many considerations; their duration, their suitability as programme music and, most important of all, their suitability as vehicles for animation. The opening piece was to be Bach's 'Toccata and Fugue in D minor'; followed by Tchaikovsky's 'Nutcracker Suite'; then Dukas' 'Sorcerer's Apprentice'; Stravinsky's 'Rite of Spring' (the 'Sacre du Printemps'); Beethoven's 'Sixth Symphony', 'The Pastoral'; Ponchielli's 'Dance of the Hours'; Moussorgsky's 'Night on Bald Mountain', and finally, Schubert's 'Ave Maria'.

Music critics were particularly scathing about Disney's treatment of Beethoven, but misunderstood Disney's aims and aspirations – *Fantasia* was designed to appeal to the audience that had applauded *Snow White*, *Pinocchio* and the *Silly Symphonies*. If it was intended as a music lesson, then the five-finger exercises were wrapped up in the Disney world of fantasy which had so far not failed him. This time, perhaps, he had overestimated his audience.

In a sense, *Fantasia* is a direct descendant of the *Silly Symphonies*, now elevated to the peerage, and was originally conceived through the agency of that familiar Disney formula, the European folk tale. 'Der Zauberlehrling', Goethe's interpretation of the old Greek story about the sorcerer's apprentice, had also been interpreted in the form of a scherzo, by Paul Dukas. The piece is brilliant and volatile with

134

192

strong rhythmic passages, and sweeping melodic phrases, perfect for animation and, thought Disney, ideal as a comic vehicle for Mickey Mouse, who seemed on the point of retiring.

MAKE MINE MUSIC

Mickey had recently appeared in the excellent short *Tugboat Mickey* (though the real star of the film is Goofy, who gets shut in the ship's gas-filled boiler, and to see more clearly strikes a match... 'Aw — gosh!') but Mickey was being constantly upstaged by Donald Duck. Walt decided that Mickey should make a comeback — alone — as 'The Sorcerer's Apprentice'.

Walt Disney's collaboration on this new project with the famous conductor Leopold Stokowski is often attributed to a chance meeting, but Disney may have engineered it, since Stokowski was already a seasoned contributor to movies. He had starred with Deanna Durbin in *100 Men and a Girl*, featuring music by Liszt, Wagner, Mozart and Verdi. In *The Big Broadcast of 1937* Stokowski had competed against Benny Goodman's 'Bugle Call Rag' with an arrangement of Bach's 'G minor Fugue'. His expertise was thus invaluable, and Disney was delighted when Stokowski offered to conduct Dukas' 'Scherzo'.

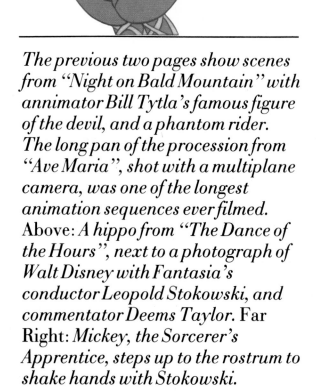

There are several accounts of how *Fantasia* grew from a short into a full-length feature film. Stokowski's genuine enthusiasm prompted him to suggest further musical experiments on film. Also, Roy Disney, with a firm hand on the studio's finances, protested that 'The Sorcerer's Apprentice' had already exceeded the budget for a short, and the balance would only be adjusted if Stokowski could be hired to make a feature film.

To Disney the possibilities of successful combinations of music and film were infinite. He invited suggestions, and Stokowski, who had made several celebrated recordings of Bach, proposed the 'Toccata and Fugue', and later, Stravinsky's 'Le Sacre du Printemps'. When the selection had been completed, Disney assigned his top animators and directors, each to a different sequence, to ensure as much variation in the style of animation as there was diversity in the music.

The structure of *Fantasia*, the combination of music and animation in a full-length feature, was unprecedented in movie history – and Walt had further innovatory ideas. *Fantasia* would be the first film to use stereophonic sound, and the first to use a wide screen, although a single attempt had been made by Abel Gance, who developed a panoramic screen in 1927.

Costs proved to be prohibitive however – even for Disney – and he dropped the idea of a wide screen

The previous two pages show scenes from "Night on Bald Mountain" with annimator Bill Tytla's famous figure of the devil, and a phantom rider. The long pan of the procession from "Ave Maria", shot with a multiplane camera, was one of the longest animation sequences ever filmed. Above: A hippo from "The Dance of the Hours", next to a photograph of Walt Disney with Fantasia's conductor Leopold Stokowski, and commentator Deems Taylor. Far Right: Mickey, the Sorcerer's Apprentice, steps up to the rostrum to shake hands with Stokowski.

to concentrate on stereophonic sound. His engineers came up with Fantasound, which employed a 35mm sound recording film, synchronized with the animated film. The sound film had several tracks, each arranged to distribute the sound through a series of loudspeakers, creating a stereophonic effect. But what of the film itself? How did it measure up to this blockbuster treatment that would eventually overrun the budget to a sprawling 2,280,000 dollars?

THEATRICAL, ABSTRACT, SURREAL

Fantasia opens with a live-action sequence, shot in silhouette against a plain background of rich colour, of the orchestra musicians, seating themselves, tuning up and waiting for their conductor. Right at the start Disney seeks to reassure his audience by having the musicians create an informal, relaxed mood, chatting and smiling to each other; this would be repeated later, between sequences. To take the highbrow edge off the film, musicians indulge in a 'jam session' during Stokowski's absence: the flute jazzes a passage from the 'Pastoral Symphony', the clarinet picks it up and turns it into Cyril Stapleton's 'Bach Goes To Town'.

Music commentator Deems Taylor introduces each sequence, explaining how the animators were inspired to create the imagery by the nature of the music. The Bach 'Toccata' evoked a semi-abstract world of violin bows and strings, flying fish, clouds, reflections on water. Styles vary from the theatrical, through abstract to the surreal, touching on the influence of Miro and Kandinsky with a nod of acknowledgement towards the popular Art Deco of the period.

Mindful of the ecclesiastical origin of the music (Bach composed for the church organ), the abstract patterns of starbursts and vapour trails pass through heavenly arches and gothic windows, terminating in a sunrise with Leopold Stokowski on his rostrum – the fantasy emanates, as all fantasies must, from the unconscious as well as the conscious.

With Tchaikovsky's 'Nutcracker Suite' we are back in the familiar world of Walt Disney with animated fairies gliding in and out of blue foliage. A group of pink-capped mushrooms tilt their heads to reveal oriental faces, and they bounce cheerfully through the 'Chinese Dance', a wonderfully inventive piece of animation, some would say *the* piece of animation, by Art Babbitt and Jules Engel.

The remainder of the 'Nutcracker' takes us through to the 'Waltz of the Flowers', via a wonderful 'Cossack Dance', an animation job given to Bill Tytla, because he was a great animator and because he came from the Ukraine.

LIVE ACTION REFERENCE

The next sequence is the focal point of the entire

Above: *Original sketch for Mickey as The Sorcerer's Apprentice.* Right: *An original sketch for Bambi.*

film – 'The Sorcerer's Apprentice'. Mickey Mouse is the Apprentice, who tries to imitate the Sorcerer's craft and is transported to limitless heights of fantasy only to find himself in deep water. He is about to drown in an almost Biblical flood created by the non-stop automated brooms fetching pails of water, when the Sorcerer comes to his aid. Mickey, chastised, hastens to clear up the debris.

The Sorcerer, 'Yensid', is of course 'Disney' spelt backwards, and the animation is faultless. Preston Blair, who worked on the film, remembers how they hired an athlete from UCLA who was urged to make a floundering, wildly unathletic leap over a pile of barrels and boxes so that the animators could study this live-action reference and animate a figure floundering in water. 'Live-action reference', said Blair, 'is a very vital part of great feature films, like all the Disney classics'. Animator Ugo D'Orsi studied the action of tumbling, thrashing water until he

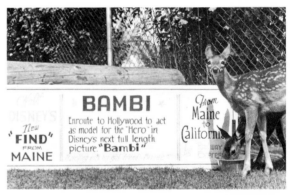

Bambi combined finely observed naturalism with caricature. To obtain the essential characteristics of deer in motion, Disney arranged for animators to attend special art classes, and had live animals brought down from Maine.

could draw it from memory.

The art of animation depends, as much as everything, on a keen eye and the observation of seemingly insignificant detail: veteran animator Art Babbitt described how it was important to get a feeling of weight to emphasise reality.

'Often an animator will draw a figure walking, and accent the foot meeting the ground as the actual step. But the step happens when the weight of the body comes down and your leg bends – *that* is your accent.'

The shift of weight, and the well-known 'squash and stretch' technique, is all part of the animator's vocabulary, wittily featured in Ponchielli's 'Dance of the Hours', where the animators used another live action reference of ballet dancers, to animate the pirouetting ostriches, hippos and alligators.

'Sorcerer' was followed, after an orchestral interim, by Stravinsky's 'Rite of Spring'. It says much for Disney's skill at presentation that he could persuade an audience to sit through this decidedly avant-garde piece. At the first performance in Paris in 1913, a scandalised audience all but threw eggs at the orchestra, the pagan rhythms offending ears that were just accepting Ravel and Debussy.

REX TAKES A BOW

Disney decided that 'Le Sacre' represented the creation of the world according to science, depicting

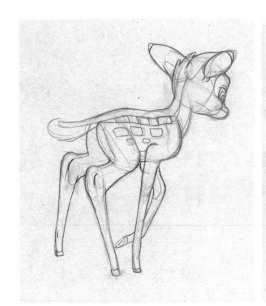

the cataclysmic upheavals that shaped the earth's crust. Stravinsky, on seeing the film, reportedly said, 'I suppose that's what I meant...' The sequence has some memorable moments: the doomed dinosaurs, huge herbivores feeding in the swamps, are alerted by a danger they sense but cannot see. The threat in this primeval paradise is conveyed by Disney's belief that menace should strike, as in the later *Bambi*, when happiness, or peace, is thoroughly established.

In the original script, the sequence is described thus:

> 'Duckbill – grabs grass under water, comes out chewing.
> Plateos digging for clams in sand. Kannemeyeria steals clam as Plateos look up – go back digging.
> Mother Diplo and babies with Navajos in foreground and other animals in background feeding – all look up.
> Diplos raise heads from water.
> Parasols feeding – look up.
> Stegosaurus looks up.
> Parrotbeak feeding – looks up.
> Dimetro looks up.
> Struthios feeding – look up.
> Triceratops feeding – looks up. Zoom pan over to ...'

This sequence matches a suitably tense passage in Stravinsky's music, and what we zoom to is a close-up of a fearsome, red-jawed carnivore, Tyrannosaurus Rex standing silhouetted against lightning flashes.

REGAINS BALANCE MOMENTARILY —

BAMBI FALLS SUDDENLY

144

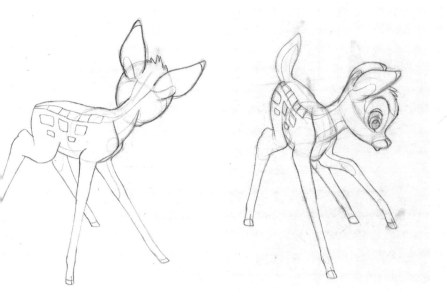

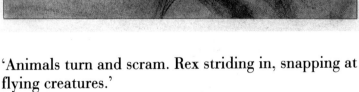

The realism of "Bambi" was a challenge to background artists and animators alike. The latter made hundreds of sketches and action sequences accurately drawn from life, some spending over an hour per drawing. Walt told his animators, "Don't show me anything until you are satisfied with it."

'Animals turn and scram. Rex striding in, snapping at flying creatures.'

Rex kills the cumbersome Stegosaurus in a fight reminiscent of *King Kong*, but is in turn overtaken by natural events as a period of intense heat turns the earth into an arid desert, and the creatures – the weak and the strong – all perish. The 'Rite of Spring' ends with an earthquake which heralds a new era.

PASTORAL AND NAIVE

An orchestral interim demonstrates the workings of the sound track in a visual interpretation, and

Beethoven's 'Pastoral Symphony' follows to give comic and rustic relief. Disney chose an Arcadian setting for this piece, and in the Storm sequence, Zeus appears in the clouds and has Hephaestus make him some thunderbolts, with which he amuses himself, hurling them at Bacchus who is fleeing on a donkey, while centaurs and centaurettes take shelter from the rain.

True, it is cute, coy, and the centaurettes are naively co-ed. There are fauns, matchmaking cupids and a doe-eyed Pegasus family, but the mythological, Attic setting allows a certain breadth of fantasy that might have been absent from comparable revels in the Vienna Woods of Beethoven's

The deer in "Bambi" look more realistic than those in earlier Disney films, thanks to the research done by the artists.

time. Beethoven himself, brooding over a glass of wine in the corner of a cafe, might have approved and echoed Stravinsky's words, 'Perhaps that's what I meant...' Disney's interpretation of the 'Pastoral Symphony' is decidedly pastoral, and naive in the way that peasant frolics might be thought naive. Ponchielli's 'Dance of the Hours', already mentioned, precedes Moussorgsky's 'Night on Bald Mountain' and Schubert's 'Ave Maria' – described by Deems Taylor as 'the struggle between the profane and the sacred'. We zoom over the rooftops of a Gothic-style town at night, and follow the Walpurgis revels of ghosts, witches, devils and skeletons, who assemble at the command of Satan on Bald Mountain.

The figure of Satan is perhaps the most memorable character in the entire film. Disney chose one of the greatest of all animators, Vladimir 'Bill' Tytla, to create and breathe life into the monstrous figure, which Tytla did with stunning effect. Bela Lugosi, famed for his portrayal of Dracula, was filmed for

live-action reference by James Wong Howe, and a model of the Devil was sculpted for Tytla to study.

The Devil and his revellers snatch a few hours of libidinous sorcery before dawn breaks, and sanity – and sanctity – is restored by a chorus of nuns in procession, singing Schubert's 'Ave Maria'. An extraordinarily long panning shot, followed by a multiplane camera tracking shot as we follow the procession into a forest designed as a church interior, is one of the triumphs of animation history.

The picture was not a success, at least in financial terms, and it would seem that Disney had temporarily lost the common touch for the first time in his career. Today, *Fantasia*, besides being accepted worldwide as a classic, plays to audiences in 'art houses', a fate that Walt Disney claims he would have deplored.

Top left: *Layout artist Joe Stahley works on an action sequence.* Below: *A team of artists headed by Tom Codrick designed the forest scenes for the film.* Above, left: *Animator Bill Justice working on story sketches for the rabbit Thumper.* Above: *Animation drawing of the owl, and a preliminary sketch for Thumper.*

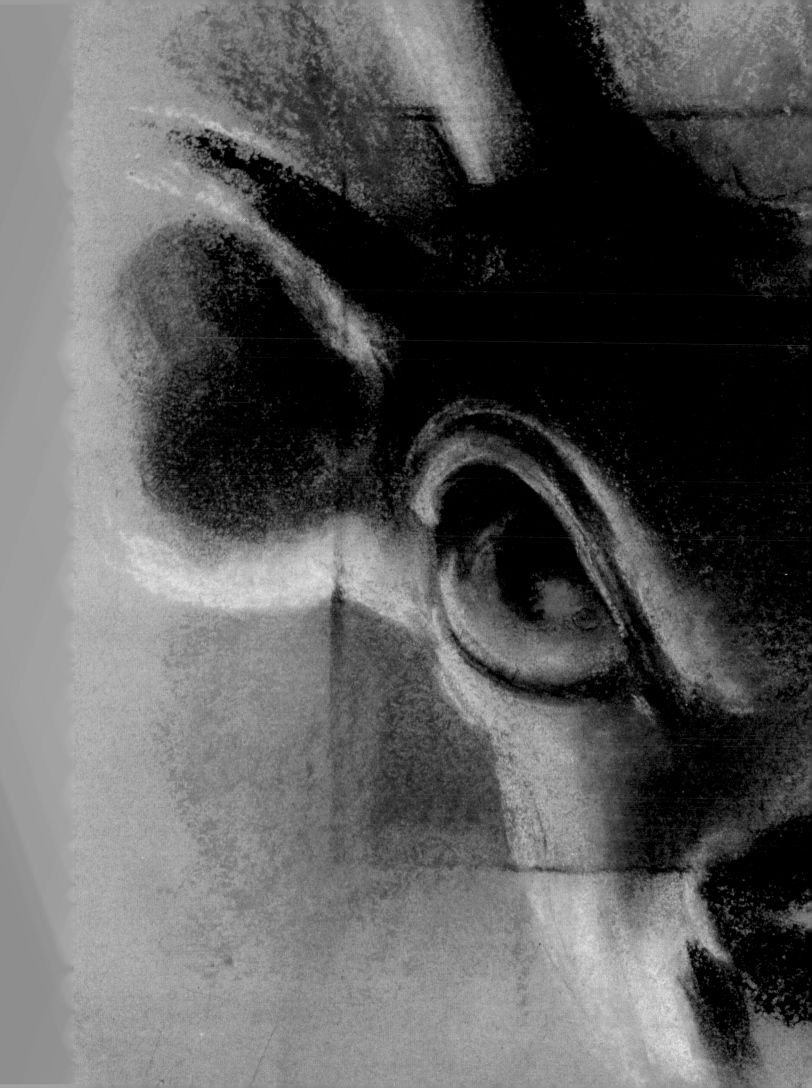

Intensely dramatic situations in "Bambi" helped the film win critical approval.

TRUE AIM

The Disney films of the late 1930s and early 1940s can be compared to a naval broadside, where all the big guns are discharged at once. *Snow White*, *Pinocchio* and *Fantasia* were soon followed by *Dumbo* and *Bambi*.

Cartoon shorts were regularly produced at this time – Pluto and Mickey Mouse picked up an Academy Award in 1941 for *Lend a Paw* and Donald Duck was nominated for *Truant Officer Donald*. It is also fair to mention that other studios were producing shorts of great merit: Walter Lantz with the crazed *Woody Woodpecker*, MGM with *Tom and Jerry* created by the Hanna-Barbera team, and Warner's *Bugs* (What's up Doc?) *Bunny*.

Bambi is a masterpiece, and as Disney commented when he saw the first rough animation sketches, 'Fellas, this is pure gold'. Disney had purchased the rights to Felix Salten's book about man's unheeding destruction of a forest and its wildlife, and had actually begun production in 1937, although *Bambi* was not released until 1942.

This gentle film needed great perseverance and research to create naturalistic backgrounds and truly animal-like animation devoid of caricature and exaggeration. Author Christopher Finch, in 'The Art of Walt Disney', pointed out the discrepancies between the Disney mainstream comic animals, such as the rabbit Thumper, and the film's aims for

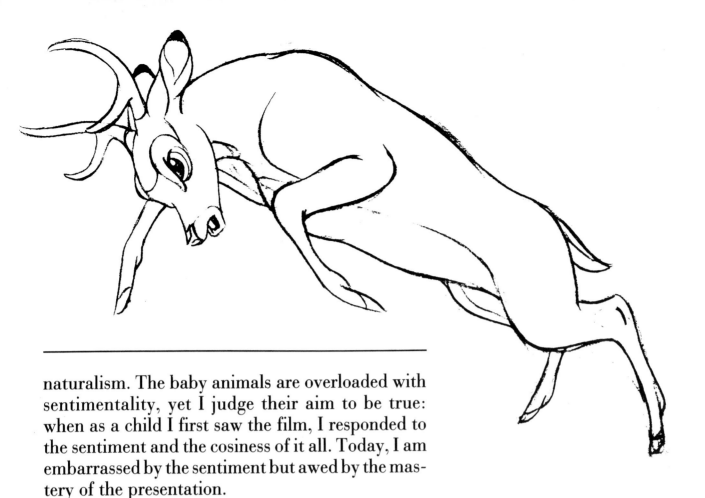

naturalism. The baby animals are overloaded with sentimentality, yet I judge their aim to be true: when as a child I first saw the film, I responded to the sentiment and the cosiness of it all. Today, I am embarrassed by the sentiment but awed by the mastery of the presentation.

FORTY-FIVE SHADES OF GREEN

Bambi opens on a long pan across a forest in grey-green and blue muted colours. It seems that the camera must have travelled for miles before we spot an owl gliding through the trees – sharp-eyed viewers may also spot reflection from the glass plates in this multiplane sequence. The drawings of the backgrounds and the animals, especially the preparatory working sketches, are exquisite, due in part to the fact that special art classes were held, using live deer as models, for the artists at work on the film. This no-stone-unturned approach was typical of Disney, and when the French biographer Maurice Bessy met Walt Disney in 1951, Walt took him to the colour laboratory, where pigments are ground and made into paints. 'Look at my greens for tree leaves,' he said, 'we now have forty-five shades'.

The *Bambi* art classes were organised by a well-known animal artist, Rico Le Brun, who helped to assemble menageries for study, while a cameraman went to Maine to film a forest during the changing

154

Left: *Background paintings for "Bambi", introducing an atmospheric, naturalistic style never previously attempted, except for the short cartoon, "The Old Mill".*
Above: *The serious mood of the film is relieved by the supporting characters, such as Thumper.*

seasons. This live-action reference footage of rain-storms, snow and waterfalls, paid off in the end. The storm sequence that follows the 'Little April Shower' song was the sort of challenge the Disney animators loved. They had created an inspired storm in *The Old Mill*, and later in the 'Pastoral Symphony', but in *Bambi* the expressive freedom of the animation is worthy of Hokusai: a mountain stream in a great hurry dashes against the rocks in its path, where individual droplets are actually *highlighted* by flashes of lightning.

Live action reference also helped in the creation of character, especially where established actors were used; the owl in *Bambi* has mannerisms strongly reminiscent of such character actors as Guy Kibbee or Eugene Pallette.

The newborn Bambi, somewhat unsteady on his

Above: *Although the film had its violent moments — the death of Bambi's mother and the forest fire — its gentle, pastoral description of life in the forest failed to have sufficient appeal to Disney audiences. It was too introspective, but "Dumbo" (right) fared much better.*

legs, is introduced to the forest creatures – quails, songbirds, rabbits, skunks, as he gradually learns to walk, and adapts to the ways of the forest. The Disney animators created an Arcadian, sylvan setting for the story, the cosiness of which emphasises its atmosphere of love and security, but also the menace which will surely follow. Disney's dramatic formula of security/fear and flight/salvation/jollity here provides a successful working structure which carries the story to its conclusion.

After the wonderful storm scene, birds shake themselves dry and sing a joyful chorus, but menace is hinted at when Bambi and his mother venture out into the open meadow, where there is no cover. Here, he first encounters his father, the 'Great Prince of the Forest', who pauses to look down at the awe-struck Bambi as he strides majestically by. Suddenly, the deer and the forest creatures take flight. Shots are heard, and the terrified Bambi, followed by his mother, dashes for the safety of trees. Later, his mother explains: 'Man,' she says, 'was in the forest...'

A tranquil sequence, set in the winter snow, lulls us once again into false security. Snow? Bambi's mother explains, 'Winter has come.' Winter leads into spring, and at the edge of the forest, on the meadow, the first spring grass pushes up through the mantle of lacy snow. We are now warned by a change in the tone of the music, which becomes

sombre, then threatening. The tempting grass dulls the edge of perception, and too late Bambi's mother senses danger. She turns to dash back into the forest, urging Bambi to 'Run...run!'

Bambi's mother is shot and killed by the hunters, and the fawn's grief and bewilderment is shown in a poignant sequence which moves audiences to tears – *Bambi* is a film of powerful realism about the joy – and the pain – of growing up, as seen through the eyes of a child. The animals in *Bambi* are surrogate humans, and share our frailty and vulnerability. This may be difficult to reconcile, since the animals are menaced and some slaughtered by man the hunter, but – and this is important – we never see the actual hunters; their presence and their threat is evoked through the music, the warnings of Bambi's parents, and the shots from their guns. It is not nature that is red in tooth and claw, but mankind. As a film, and as entertainment, *Bambi* is perhaps too real and too salutary for adults and children alike.

Part of the appeal of Disney feature films lies in Walt's strong sense of melodrama skilfully pack-

Dumbo, the baby elephant with the outsize ears. Above, left: *Animator Bill Reed works on a preliminary sketch.* Right: *Two of the malicious gossips about to go into orbit.*

158

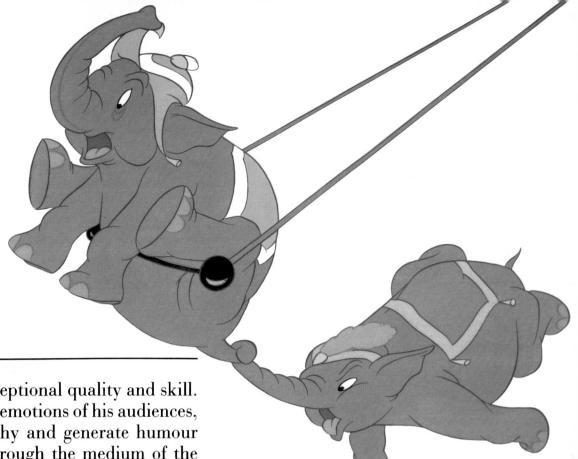

aged in animation of exceptional quality and skill. Walt liked to play on the emotions of his audiences, to capture their sympathy and generate humour and inspire concern. Through the medium of the cartoon film, and by using animals as the main characters, Disney induced the audience to identify with the principal – and most sympathetic – participants in the story. It is *because* they are animals that we can more readily acknowledge them and feel empathy. Anthropomorphic fantasy relies, in part, on the relationship of the child to the world of animals. Children – and many adults – quickly respond to the cosy, unaffected and simple world of animals, and when they are endowed with human characteristics and adopt human voices, then the fantasy becomes intensified, a condition that is only possible through the medium of the cartoon film. In Bambi's world there are no animal predators, so that the menace of man, when he arrives, is even more sharply defined.

Disney's last animated film, *The Jungle Book*, made 25 years after Bambi, puts humans and animals on much the same level by introducing the child Mowgli, who has been reared by wolves. Mowgli possesses all the characteristics of a normal, mischievous boy, except that his companions are animals and he talks their language, or rather, they talk ours, and are skilled at human mimicry. Here, the menacing predator is a tiger with the voice and the mannerisms of a smooth-tongued and crooked politician. Mowgli is urged by the other jungle animals to return to civilisation and human society, to escape from the tiger. Where *Bambi* aimed at realism, and provided minimal comic relief, in *The Jungle Book* humour is stoutly maintained throughout, though the fantasy is retained. It was a formula that Disney had established right at the outset of his career in feature films with *Snow White* where the menace of the wicked Queen is alleviated by the humour of the dwarfs, and in the end it is they who, quite literally, precipitate her downfall.

TOO ECCENTRIC—TOO SERIOUS

Neither *Pinocchio* nor *Fantasia* had enjoyed the huge success of *Snow White and the Seven Dwarfs*, and *Bambi* didn't exactly romp home. It is hard to say exactly why these later films failed to measure up to *Snow White*. During the production of *Pinocchio*, the Disney brothers had realised that expansion was inevitable, and moved out of the old, homely Hyperion building to a new site at Burbank, at a cost of some three million dollars. Furthermore, the production costs of *Pinocchio*, *Fantasia* and *Bambi* had swallowed the profits made by *Snow White*, not to mention the short films, and the fact that two other features were being processed along with *Bambi*. These were *Dumbo*, and *The Reluctant Dragon*.

Far left: *Animator Fred Moore and friend.* Left: *Director Jack Kinney with singer Cliff Edwards.* Above: *One of animator Ward Kimball's crows, a composite parody of black entertainers of the 1930s.*

One might speculate that part of *Snow White's* success was due to its novelty, being the first cartoon feature, and that *Pinocchio* failed in the way that a second novel often fails, because the author has put all his – or her – eggs in one basket; that

Fantasia was too eccentric and *Bambi* too serious and lyrical. Furthermore, the movie industry was facing one of the worst slumps in its history, and attendance had dropped from 85 million to 55 million by 1941 – a Gallup poll discovered that people actually preferred listening to the radio than going to the movies, also that the audience's favourite movie star was – wait for it – Mickey Rooney, in such features as *Babes on Broadway*.

All these factors contributed to some extent to the fact that the later films couldn't quite measure up to the success of the most famous animated feature film of all time. But the principle reason may be that *Snow White and the Seven Dwarfs* was a romance, a

Preliminary sketches and backgrounds for "Dumbo". Top right: *Animation drawing of the crows.*

boy and girl fairytale that contained exactly the right ingredients. The story is simple with a strong element of symbolism. *Pinocchio*, on the other hand, is quite a complex plot involving many adventures, in the course of which we meet a variety of diverse characters. *Fantasia* was too intellectual, though rich in its change of mood, and *Bambi* was too introspective. They may even be *too good*, too brilliant, in terms of technicality and animation; so much attention to detail was lavished on *Pinocchio* and *Bambi* that the films are rather slow in getting to the point of the story, where a broader canvas would have been more appropriate.

In the future, animation could be bolder, sketchier, cruder or, God forbid, psychedelic, but it would never be finer. The Disney artists had made a definite statement.

WHEN I SEE AN ELEPHANT FLY

In terms of profit and popularity, the most successful Disney film since *Snow White* was the short and sweet *Dumbo*, an awkward, baby elephant with oversize ears — a circus freak in fact. Dumbo's birth is overdue, and he is eventually brought to his anxious mother by a stork, voiced by the actor Sterling Holloway. The stork has to rest periodically on a cloud, to consult a map and get his bearings — 'Up to the gas station and turn left...' With *Dumbo* we are once again back with mainstream Disney in

163

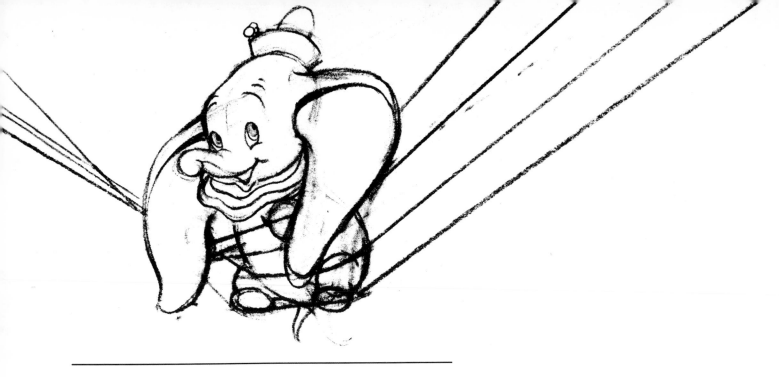

Cartoon-land, although the story — by Harold Pearl and Helen Aberson — has much in common with *Pinocchio*; like him, baby Dumbo is obliged to endure adversity and adventure en route to acceptance and recognition. Pinocchio undergoes a moral cleansing, asses' ears and a long nose to become a real boy, while Dumbo endures separation from his mother — when she sings 'Baby Mine' — and the harsh circus life to win fame and fortune as a flying elephant. As a cartoon feature, *Dumbo* combines all the right qualities of the successful American musical. The erecting of circus tents and the big top at night, in the pouring rain, gives the scene a sense of urgency and rhythm, assisted by the music. The gags are vintage Disney: the circus gorilla, showing off by tugging fiercely at the bars of his cage, is embarrassed when a bar comes loose — shame-facedly he replaces it.

The female elephants that form the circus troupe are a wonderfully catty bunch, and their come-uppance — or more accurately their downfall from the heights of the circus tent is an eagerly awaited and satisfying event as a collapsing pyramid of pachyderm.

As in many of Disney's feature films there are highlights that become, in time, regarded as classic models of animation: Bill Tytla's gossipy elephants, ('Girls — have I got a trunkful of dirt...) the quartet of crows who sing 'When I see an elephant fly', animated by Ward Kimball and influenced, no doubt, by black scat singers such as Cab Calloway; the sequence where Dumbo and his friend Timothy Mouse, get drunk and see 'Pink Elephants on Parade', voiced by Ed Brophy, a famous sequence that must have inspired Colonel Hathi's Elephant Patrol in *The Jungle Book*. The scene was perhaps in turn inspired by Art Babbitt's drinking sequence in *The Country Cousin*, 1936. Apparently Babbitt asked Walt if he could have some expenses for research, so that he could get drunk 'to know what it feels like.' Animators on *Dumbo* included Bill Tytla, Ward Kimball, Karl Van Leuven and Norm Ferguson, and by all accounts they enjoyed themselves, especially on the brilliantly inventive 'Pink Elephants': after a celebration drink of champagne a group of circus clowns throw a half-full bottle into a tub of water. Dumbo drinks from the tub and Timothy Mouse actually falls in. The champagne has an immediate effect – Dumbo blows a trunk-shaped bubble. 'Can you do a square one?' asks Timothy. Dumbo obliges, and follows with a gigantic bubble that separates to become a troop of marching pink elephants. These transform themselves into devil elephants, ghost elephants, a camel-elephant, a pyramid elephant, and elephants striped, spotted and checkered. A pink elephant divides into two, and they use their trunks to generate an arc of electricity between them.

Person-to-person – Dumbo and friend Timothy Mouse, whose voice-over was brilliantly done by character actor Ed Brophy, seen above with animators Norman Ferguson (left) and John Lounsbery. Ferguson, with Karl Van Leuven, Hick Lokey, Howard Swift, and Ken O'Connor did the memorable scene, "Pink Elephants on Parade".

In spite of the top talent employed on *Dumbo*, director Ben Sharpsteen was urged to keep costs down and minimise special effects. The film was short and simple, and its appeal to audiences was realised when it earned a profit of 850,000 dollars.

REAPING REWARDS

The success of *Dumbo* was offset by *The Reluctant Dragon*, released in 1941, which failed to make a profit. The film is a curiosity and a departure from the usual Disney format. *The Reluctant Dragon* is a hybrid of three short cartoons linked together by a live-action documentary, featuring the humorist Robert Benchley, who is shown the workings of the Disney studios in Burbank.

In 1938 a theatre manager in Pittston, PA, had written to Walt Disney, informing Disney that he had carried out a survey among his patrons, and only three of these people had but the vaguest idea of how cartoons were made – most thought that Disney used automatons or dolls, a conviction no doubt reinforced after *Pinocchio* was released.

The Reluctant Dragon, aside from being a vehicle for the three shorts, *Baby Weems*, *How to Ride a Horse*, and *The Reluctant Dragon*, was also an exercise in public relations and promotions, rather than an altruistic desire on the part of Disney to give lessons in film making. It is a clever, well-made film that sustains our interest to the end, and it may have

Right: *The infant prodigy Baby Weems, one of the short cartoons from the feature, "The Reluctant Dragon", a live-action vehicle for humorist Robert Benchley.*

166

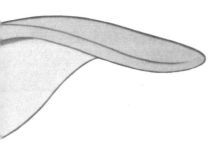

had a less obvious purpose. Possibly, Disney felt that he was reaping all the rewards, and all the glory while his staff remained in the background.

But if *The Reluctant Dragon* aimed to show the harmonious relationship enjoyed between Walt and the studio, and allowed him to share some of the limelight with his animators, the discontent that was to lead to strike action and unionisation would show that it was already too late. The halcyon days that had begun with the old Hyperion Studio were at an end.

Walt Disney's dedication to his work, on the other hand, continued to be entirely selfless. He became known as the 'hardest worker in Hollywood', single-minded to the point of obsession. His ceaseless drive took him to the studio at dawn – on those days when he spent the night at home instead of at the studio. In the evening, after the animators had left, Disney roamed the studios, peering at work pinned on animator's desks, rummaging in wastepaper baskets for rejected drawings, which he sometimes insisted were re-instated. He was often short-tempered, sharp-tongued, his sense of humour found wanting. Disney was feared by some, and accused of being despotic: Maurice Bessy told Walt he was a 'Fuhrer', yet Disney could be generous, warm-hearted and sympathetic. He once referred to himself as 'the last of the benevolent monarchs'. He was particularly courteous to the

Walt Disney welcomes Benchley to the Burbank studio. Benchley's tour of the studio was the subject of the film, which linked together three cartoons: "Baby Weems", "How to Ride a Horse", and the title cartoon, "The Reluctant Dragon". Right: Benchley and Frances Gifford visit the Paint Lab, and artist T. Hee.

lower-echelon members of his staff, the carpenters,
electricians and chauffeurs. It is not generally

Two levels from the multiplane camera for "So Dear to My Heart", the top level on glass. The picture right shows the effect when the two paintings are shot through the multiplane camera.

known that each Christmas, Disney entertained children at the hospital opposite the studios, performing acts with glove puppets, and when he died in 1966, some staff members went around openly weeping. Disney had inherited, for better or for worse, many of his father's characteristics, which included a large measure of naivety, and insensitivity to the aims of others.

Inevitably, reports on Disney's behaviour conflict. Some say that he was incapable of firing people, while others assert that hiring and firing was a regular pattern at Disney's: one gag-writer was fired on the spot (and later allowed to return) because he told Walt that 'he wouldn't know a funny story if it jumped up and bit him.'

Benchley and Gifford visit the Camera Department; the filming of a sweatbox scene featuring Walt.

Although there were bonuses for successes, for contributions to stories, gags and ideas, animators often had to work very long hours, and felt themselves underpaid, especially since it was common knowledge that some actors and actresses were receiving a princely 6,000 dollars a week, compared to an animator's several hundred. Even so, story men, gag writers and animators were always included in the movie credits, and although an Oscar 'might wind up in Walt's office' it might also have your name engraved on the base. If Disney took the credit, he also shouldered, along with Roy Disney, all the worries, and all the decisions. I. Klein recalls that:

> 'At the end it was Disney's decision, like a Roman Emperor at the gladiator combat arena...thumbs up or thumbs down...'

Benchley visits an art class and examines sound effects of baby cries.

CHAPTER SEVEN

HAPPILY EVER AFTER

EVENTUALLY, IT WAS THE WORKERS who gave the thumbs down to Disney. They did not share his almost missionary zeal and dedication to the art and craft of the cartoon. Sure, they wanted their work to be recognized as the finest in the business, but there were other things in life. When unionism arrived in Hollywood, during the late 1930s and early '40s, union leaders found many willing recruits at Burbank, and the Disney studio went on strike, with animators picketing outside the gates.

The strike, a bitter blow to Disney's pride and ideals, co-incided with America's entry into the Second World War, and both events robbed Disney of some of his finest animators, including Bill Tytla and Art Babbitt (a key figure in the strike).

The Disney feature films of the war years were not exactly inspired by the Disney fantasy – perhaps the harsh reality of the strike, the considerable loss of overseas revenue, plus the shortages of film material had robbed him of inspiration, if not dedication to duty.

The Disney studio turned out numerous documentary and instructional films using animation techniques. They produced the well-known *Victory*

José Carioca was a symbol of Disney's South American films.

Through Air Power, based on the book by Major Alexander P. de Seversky, and featured Donald Duck in *Der Fuhrer's Face*, which contained a popular wartime song of the same title, composed by Oliver Wallace. The film had considerable propaganda value, with European translations smuggled in by the underground — much to the chagrin of Nazi High Command — and won an Academy Award in 1943. The short cartoons managed to retain much of their quality and sparkle; many had military themes — and more often were instructive — *Private Pluto*, *Victory Vehicles*, *Home Defence*, *Commando Duck* and *How to be a Sailor*.

Through 1938, Donald Duck had gradually overtaken Mickey in popularity, aided and abetted by Pluto and Goofy. Gerald Burtnett, writing in the magazine section of 'The Los Angeles Times', said of Donald Duck:

'Being born in the midst of the late depression, Donald was a child of adversity and like so many of them, made his way by squawking. The duck was always mad. Mickey was the spirit of fun and light and good moral principle. I hate to say this, but the duck seems to have won!'

'Oh, boy, oh boy!'

BIRDS OF A FEATHER

The two main features of the war years were *Salu-*

dos Amigos and *The Three Cabelleros*, which arose from a goodwill tour to Latin America, undertaken by Disney at the suggestion of the State Department at the time of the studio strike. The government offered to finance the project, and Disney chose a creative team to help gather material that was to be made into several short films, the content of which would establish a cultural *entente*.

Donald Duck was the anchor man – or rather, anchor Duck – in both *Saludos* and the *Caballeros* film, and the Disney artists created complementary characters of Latin-American aspect, such as José Carioca, a high-stepping parrot that was Brazil's answer to Donald Duck. There is Pedro, a mail plane with a personality, and a Mexican bandito disguised as a cockerel, by the name of Panchito. Donald engages in mild flirtation with some live-action ladies in *The Three Caballeros*: he also joins forces with José Carioca and Panchito, to sing the song that gave the film its title.

Animator Ward Kimball recalled that in terms of creativity, *The Three Caballeros* was a fun film to work on, and one of the most enjoyable of his career. The first postwar film with any breadth of vision was *Song of the South*, although it is worth recording that in *Fun and Fancy Free* a 'package' film containing a Mickey Mouse featurette, *Mickey and the Beanstalk*, Jim Macdonald takes over from Walt as the voice of Mickey Mouse, a service that

Far Left: *Walt Disney on his tour of Latin America, 1941. The outcome of the tour was the two films, "Saludos Amigos" and "The Three Caballeros". The pictures* left, *and* above, *are from "Saludos Amigos".*

Walt had performed for twenty years.

SOFT AS SPOONBREAD

Song of the South heralds the studio's return to American folklore and grass roots, picking up the cotton threads that were put aside during the 1940s. Production budgets could not bear the expense of a wholly animated feature, so Disney settled for a compromise, and balanced a live-action story with the cartoon inserts. The story is based on that of Joel Chandler Harris's 'Uncle Remus' tales, of a surely idealised life on a southern plantation.

Bobby Driscoll plays the little boy from the plantation house, who sits at the feet of the wise old story teller, Uncle Remus, played by James Baskett, to absorb the adventures of the make-believe Br'er Rabbit and Br'er Fox. The fox and the rabbit are, of course, animated in the finest Disney tradition. Disney's foxes always delight the eye and ear. The fox in *Pinocchio*, Honest John, is a wonderfully characterised con artist. The fox pursued by hounds in *Mary Poppins* is as Irish as Guinness, while the fox cast as Robin Hood has an awe-inspiring, upper-class English accent. Br'er Fox is a wacky, fast-talking, wildly animated creature with a Southern drawl (also James Baskett) dedicated to the destruction of Br'er Rabbit.

Anyone who deplored the loss of the Disney touch during the war years was fully reconciled by this

178

film. While some critics thought the live-action as soft as spoonbread, the animated sections and its hit song 'Zip-A-Dee-Doo-Dah' restored their confidence – the old Mousetro hadn't lost his touch, he'd merely mislaid it.

The features that followed *Song of the South*, released in 1946, such as *Melody Time, So Dear to my Heart* and *The Adventures of Ichabod and Mr. Toad*, the latter extracted from Kenneth Grahame's 'The Wind in the Willows', were mere stepping stones to the 1950 film of *Cinderella*.

The magic, glass-slipper world of *Cinderella* is

"One of those Zip-A-Dee-Doo-Dah days." "Song of the South" was based on the Uncle Remus, Br'er Rabbit stories, featuring actor James Baskett (above) *in live-action sequences sandwiched between the Br'er Rabbit cartoons.*

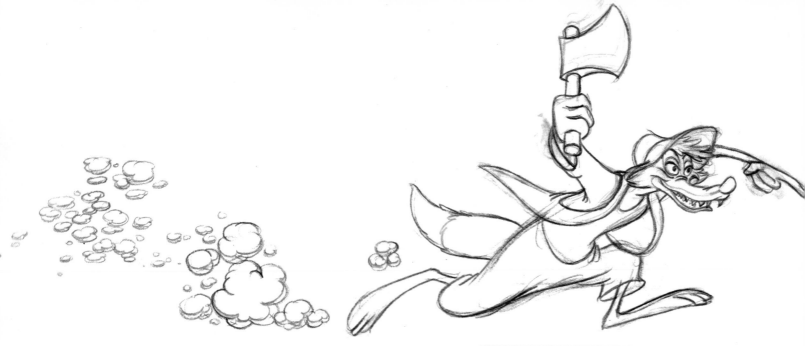

conveyed right at the start of the film as the camera tracks in to a close-up of the book, which opens on the title. Disney used this popular and comfortable device in many films – *Pinocchio*, *Robin Hood*, *Davy Crockett* – to establish the fireside world of the fairytale and the adventure story. *Song of the South* actually employs a flickering, open hearth and a gently rocking chair to give extra credence to the storyteller, Uncle Remus.

THE LEGACY OF CINDERELLA

Cinderella has much in common with the earlier *Snow White*, the fairy castle – in *Cinderella* a magnificent and romantic structure with an incandescent glow – the cruel stepmother, the creatures that befriend her, a Ruritanian prince, plus the essential ingredient of at least one hit song. The Fairy Godmother's song, 'Bibbidi-Bobbidi-Boo' provided the hit, backed up by 'So This is Love'. Thirteen years separated the two features and the advances in animation techniques and the style of the artwork is very evident; *Cinderella* is crisper, and with flat areas of colour. Some of the backgrounds owe something to the illustration styles of the period, although the influence that Disney has had on graphic design is considerable.

Cinderella was a great success, for it achieved an almost perfect balance of humour (provided by the mice, Jaq and Gus) with the romance. Ub Iwerks

Above: *Br'er Fox, and scenes from "Song of the South". Br'er Fox, for variety, is here pursuing the White Rabbit from Disney's "Alice in Wonderland".*

who had returned to the studio in 1940 did the special effects, and Ben Sharpsteen directed. In one respect, success is inherent in the story, since almost every country in the world has its own version – the story of *Cinderella* has been passed down from generation to generation for hundreds of years.

Cinderella was closely followed by the release of

Left: *Luana Patten in "Song of the South"*. Right: *Oliver Wallace directs Kathy Beaumont's singing as "Alice" and she acts with Ed Wynn for the live action cameras.*

Trump card troops from the final scenes of "Alice". Disney was more at home with Grimm's peasant folklore than Carroll's whimsical, English fantasy, but the cartoon has some fine moments.

two modern classics, *Alice in Wonderland* (1951) and *Peter Pan* (1953), and in 1959 the old fairytale of *Sleeping Beauty*. Walt Disney was intent on re-establishing his reputation as a master storyteller while playing safe with well-loved stories, although he had been tempted by Lewis Carroll's story of Alice since 1933.

The trouble with 'Alice' is that the story has little elbow room for anyone else's fantasy or contribution other than the author's. A strong visual identity had already been established by Tenniel's famous illustrations, which the studio once considered utilising, and in addition the story is eccentric and almost mystical.

Perhaps the story was too English for the Disney treatment to work successfully, even though the animators tried to capture the surreal flavour by adding such strange figures as a dog with a brush for a head and a birdcage bird, reminiscent of Tenniel's own Bread-and-Butter flies. Lewis Carroll's 'Alice' is not a cosy story, and offers few opportunities of a 'cute' treatment, being full of unyielding and decidedly aggressive characters.

Animator and director Ward Kimball said that the inherent eccentricity in the book affected directors so that *Alice* suffered from having too many of them. Here was a case of five directors each trying to top the other guy and make his sequence the biggest and the craziest in the show. But the film has

One of the best sequences is the Mad Hatter's Tea Party, where the Disney animators have successfully captured the style of Tenniel's original drawings while retaining the Disney image.

184

some fine moments: the Mad Hatter's Tea Party is genuinely funny instead of being merely mad, while the pink-striped Cheshire Cat, inspired by Tenniel, is nonetheless pure Disney — since Julius in the early *Alice* films the breed could now boast quite a pedigree.

Alice in Wonderland took five years to make and cost around three million dollars to produce. It was not a success perhaps for the reasons proposed above — the book allows its readers to follow a private, unconscious fantasy. The film also provides one, and the two are not reconcilable.

PIXIE DUST

While *Alice* and *Peter Pan* were going through production, Walt Disney's remarkably diverse genius had been fired by the idea that was to obsess him for the rest of his life, an amusement park that would also be his vision of a sort of public Utopia. He would call it 'Disneyland'.

Accordingly, he set up an organisation and a fund, identified by his initials, WED, to turn the dream into reality. This was a revolutionary concept in every way, since the aim of the fairytale is to turn reality into a dream. Later in the chapter we will have a close look at Disneyland and the Magic Kingdoms.

Barrie's 'Peter Pan' turned the austere world of Edwardian nursery life, with its starched nannies

Above: *The English Alice, and opposite the universal Cinderella, a folk tale with at least 350 variations.* Right: *Live-action reference model of Cinderella to assist animators. Live-action reference is essential to the art of the cartoon, particularly where a considerable degree of realism is required.*

and aloof parents into an escapist fantasy. Peter Pan was in every way the ideal Disney film. This epic of boyhood had a natural appeal to Disney, for it is a fairytale spiced with adventure – Peter Pan was the boy who wouldn't grow up. The fantasy of flight is a regular element of fairy stories, but virtually impossible to put across on the stage. Disney was able to interpret Barrie's immortal play, produced in 1904, with all the techniques available to the modern cartoon-maker. In his book 'The Disney Films' Leonard Maltin points out that for the first time the play could be realised without the aid of traditional artifice. Until now Peter Pan had always been played on stage by a girl, but Walt Disney gives us a boy in Greenwood Forest attire. The crocodile and the dog Nana now come into their own, while that pixie of all pixies, Tinker Bell, who wraps Barrie's fairy world in pixie dust, is no longer a darting ball of light, but an attractive, very feminine creature.

The story has many wonderful ingredients – pirates, Indians, the menacing Captain Hook, the crocodile whose presence is betrayed by the alarm clock he has once swallowed. The idea to make *Peter Pan* into a full-length feature had occurred to Disney when *Snow White* was being produced in 1935, during the decade that Disney's creative imagination was at its peak.

Disney had discovered that in the world of the fairytale, especially the cartoon fairytale, virtually

As in "Bambi" Disney combined realism with caricature. Cinderella, the Prince, the Stepmother and her two daughters were drawn and animated from life, while Cinderella's friends, the mice and other animals, are cartoon characters. The bottom picture on the opposite page shows Ilene Woods doing Cinderella's voice-over.

anything was possible. When, during a story session on *Snow White*, the story men had told Walt that they couldn't see a way to get her to bite the poisoned 'wishing' apple, Disney said:

> 'I believe any fairy tale can have wishing things. just as the Queen can have a mirror that knows all. or that she can poison an apple and later change into an old hag. I believe these things are essential to fairytales. and the fantasy of the wish makes the girl bite into the apple. whereas she wouldn't otherwise be interested.'

SENSE OF INTIMACY

In 1959 Walt Disney released the third of the famous trio of stories. *Snow White*, *Cinderella* and now *Sleeping Beauty*. It failed to enrapture, it failed as a fantasy, and eventually failed to earn its keep — the production had cost a staggering six million, had taken six years to complete, but receipts only grossed 5.3 million. A lot of money, certainly, but not in terms of the blockbuster movie; *Sleeping*

Beauty had originally been conceived as the studio's magnum opus, the last word in advanced techniques, and splendour of presentation. Long sequences were filmed for live-action reference. The film was shot in the new Technirama 70, an improvement on Cinerama, so-called because two identical 35 mm negatives are printed as a double frame on one 70 mm strip of film and projected through an anamorphic lens, having the advantage of a wider angle of view.

This was one of the studio's most ambitious projects, with old hands such as Milt Kahl, Frank Thomas and Ollie Johnston overseeing animation, thus providing the sure Disney touch. They took no chances, and the film opens traditionally, with the turning pages of a Fairy Tale book, and faint strains of Tchaikovsky's music. The animation and art-work is very stylised, similar to a theatre backdrop; the colours vivid pinks, oranges and yellows. The style might have suited other cartoon studios, but somehow it didn't work for the Disney image, nor for the animation, in spite of long and expensive sequences with the multiplane camera, tracking through castles and forests. Looking at the film today, over twenty years later, the technique remains impressive as ever, but the style is somewhat sterile and cold.

Sleeping Beauty is anchored by links to past successes, either intentionally or otherwise: the forest

Claude Coats, Wilfred Jackson, & John Hench study sketches; photographing "Peter Pan".

animals echo those of *Snow White* and *Bambi*; there
are touches of *Fantasia*, in particular the bucket
and broom sequence ('The Sorcerer's Apprentice')
where the animated brooms clean out the forest cottage (Snow White). There are several good gags:
'Father, you are living in the past – this is the 14th

Barrie's "Peter Pan" created a magic world on the stage, but Disney's became a reality. Far Left: A plan of Disneyland during construction, with Peter Ellenshaw painting a map of Disneyland, Above: Photos show the progress from orange groves to completed park.

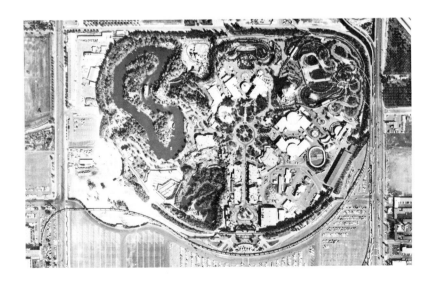

195

196

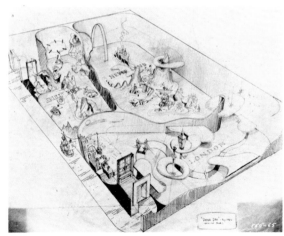

Peter Pan in Disneyland. Left: a scene from the film, the Galleon flies over Never Land. Above: The Peter Pan Ride at Disneyland; testing the controls; layout drawing of "Peter Pan Fly-Thru".

197

century...' and comic relief is supplied by the three Fairy Godmothers, plump, well-meaning busy-bodies who, at the flick of a magic wand, provide themselves with tea and cookies.

By far the most memorable and compelling character is not the winsome Sleeping Beauty, nor the cardboard Prince, but the wonderfully evil phantom Maleficent, a black-gowned, stately creature who somewhat resembles Katharine Hepburn out of Charles Addams. She and her growling, prattling Goons, aided by a cunning raven, try to bring about Beauty's death by witchcraft. Thwarted by the Prince, who comes to rescue Sleeping Beauty. Maleficent pursues him through a forest of thorns, where she turns into a monstrous, fiery dragon, black and yellow and breathing sulphurous flames. The Prince hurls a magic sword which pierces the dragon's breast, and she perishes in a scene of medieval splendour.

So why did *Sleeping Beauty*, the most expensive cartoon ever made up to that time, fail to attract a larger audience? Some critics have suggested that the fairytale had reached its limits, at least as far as the animated feature was concerned. They may have been right. UPA's first full-length cartoon feature, *1001 Arabian Nights*, with Mr. Magoo, was released in the same year, and also fared badly. Audiences had seen it all before, and were unimpressed even by the stereophonic sound and the wide

Left: *Peter Pan, and a character sketch of Captian Hook, ever fearful of the c-c-crocodile who severed his left hand.* Above: *Fugitive from "Fantasia": The model of the dinosaur Tyrannosaurus Rex comes to Disneyland on July 1, 1966.*

screen. Thus, the film had lost that vital sense of intimacy with the audience, the one-to-one cosiness that Disney injected into all of his or most of his previous films. The soft Thirties and early Forties style of artwork had given way to a stronger, less sensitive graphic style. Disney animators were influenced by — and in turn influenced — the art and illustration styles of the period, a style that would be excellent for *The Jungle Book*, *101 Dalmatians*, and the animated sequences in *Mary Poppins*, but it lacked the magical quality essential to a classic fairy story.

Perhaps the main reason for the failure of *Sleep-*

ing Beauty was the absence of Walt's undivided attention during production. Overtaken by his preoccupation with Disneyland, he was like the editor who had been suddenly called away, leaving the staff to put the paper to bed; although highly skilled, they were lost without his constant guidance and editorial flair, his dedication and genius.

RUM AND ROMANCE

Disneyland is all of Walt Disney's fantasies cast as reality, built as a film-set on a *Ben Hur* scale, neatly dovetailed into a fairy world of robust adventure and pixie-dust dreams. Many of the later films have inspired the themes underlying the various features – The Swiss Family Robinson's Tree House; Pirates of the Caribbean, a boat ride through a Yo-ho-ho and a bottle of rum underground scenario of electronically controlled figures, has a touch of *Treasure Island*. The submarine world borrows some effects from *20,000 Leagues Under the Sea*;

The pirate ship under construction, then placed in Fantasyland at Disneyland. Right: *Tinker Bell oversees construction of the Golden Horseshoe, and Walt's model train serves as a model for the Disneyland train.*

Frontierland and riverboat trip from *Davy Crockett*; the fairy castle from *Sleeping Beauty*.

Treasure Island had been released five years before the opening of Disneyland, and was the studio's first completely live-action film. It was inevitable that Disney should turn his attentions to exploit the conventional movie, and the opportunity arose when Roy Disney pointed out that there were 'frozen' assets in Britain – revenue amassed by the

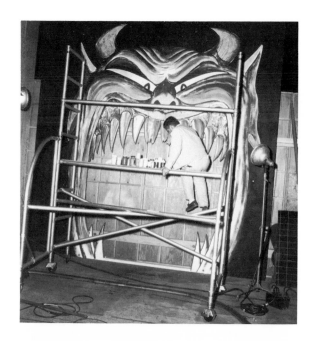

box-office receipts for Disney films that could only be spent in Britain.

Fairy stories do not lend themselves well to interpretation by the conventional movie, even in the hands of a film maker as gifted as Disney, but adventure stories laced with rum and romance on the high seas, that – if you will forgive the pun – is a different kettle of fish.

Treasure Island is an immensely enjoyable film. It managed a very rare feat – to be better than the original, something that re-makes rarely achieve, since they are forced to combat movie nostalgia and take a different approach. Disney's version follows the conventional lines of Robert Louis Stevenson's book, and so did the original film. Wallace Beery was memorable as Long John Silver – but Robert Newton's rolling-eyed, West Country, likeable villain is outstanding.

Walt Disney's *Treasure Island* also underlined a factor that is never made clear – *Treasure Island* is less a tale of a search for buried treasure than a love story – the love that grows between the boy, Jim Hawkins, and the roguish Silver. Fate had cast them on opposite sides, but they recognised their bond of courage, and both had a natural empathy for the other. Jim Hawkins was played by Bobby Driscoll, who had grown a few inches since his role in *Song of the South*, the only American in an all-British cast. *Treasure Island* cost 1,800,000 dollars, and it was worth every cent – or rather, every penny.

The balance of the funds in Britain went towards three other live-action movies, all cast in the mould of 'Boy's Own Paper' heroism and romance. These were the perennial favourite, *The Story of Robin Hood and His Merrie Men*, with Richard Todd and a very young Peter Finch; a distillation of Sir Walter Scott's *Rob Roy*, shot on location in Scotland, starring Richard Todd and actress Glynis Johns; and a Tudor romance, *The Sword and the Rose*, which also starred Richard Todd and Glynis Johns against James Robertson Justice's Henry VIII. The breakaway from the animated film encouraged Disney to exploit the medium further and make some remarkable nature features.

UPSTAGED BY A SQUID

Two years before *Treasure Island* was released, cinema audiences saw *Seal Island*, filmed by Alaskan Al Milotte and his wife Elma, the first of the True Life Adventure Series, which won an Academy Award. Disney was again breaking new ground – movie makers had never dared to risk a nature subject on a full-length feature, unless you count the quaint, British wartime film *Tawny Pipit*, the story of a bird-watching Battle of Britain pilot.

The success of *Seal Island* was followed by a lot of similar projects, including *The Living Desert*, *The*

Craftsmen of all fields lent their talents to building Disneyland's attractions. Where else would you see a hippo, a mountain and a submarine taking shape?

Left: *Cinderella's Castle at Walt Disney World, Florida.* Above: *Tinker Bell peers through the keyhole, and Walt Disney surveys a model of his Magic Kingdom.*

Vanishing Prairie and *The African Lion*. The films were shot and edited with the painstaking care and attention to detail inherent in animated films, and the scenes of nature red in tooth and claw from *The Living Desert* are memorable.

Two men were responsible for Disney's most extravagent live-action movie of the 1950s, adapted from Jules Verne's science-fiction adventure, *20,000 Leagues Under The Sea*, released on Christmas Eve 1954. Card Walker and Bill Walsh had been exploring the possibilities of a marine life nature film, but the subject turned out to have more exciting opportunities. *20,000 Leagues* is a wonderful adventure story, with all the ingredients: a mad Captain, a giant squid, a cataclysmic finale — sufficient to keep the special effects department happy for years.

Ub Iwerks was in charge of the mattes, which enable technicians to shoot two different action sequences and superimpose them in register. In addition, glass paintings and rear-screen projections were used, and it was planned to shoot the film in Cinemascope. Disney chose as his director the young Richard Fleischer, son of the cartoon maker, Max Fleischer, and hired an impressive cast: James Mason as Captain Nemo, Kirk Douglas to play Ned Land the harpooner, Paul Lukas as Professor Aronnax, and the inimitable Peter Lorre as Conseil, the Professor's assistant. But the performer that really

stole the show was the giant squid built by special effects technician Robert Mattey, who went on to construct the shark in *Jaws*. Two veteran movies, De Mille's *Reap the Wild Wind* and Rank's *The Blue Lagoon* have famous fight sequences with giant squids, but they are mere inkfish when compared to Disney's octopus.

It was also the most expensive, costing around 250,000 dollars, to create this two-ton, hydraulically operated monster, some fifty feet long, which was worked by a team of twenty-eight men. Sequences were shot with a special underwater camera, and a crew of operators in scuba equipment. The prototype became waterlogged and sank.

The second squid was more robust and convincing, but the scene was filmed at sunset on a calm sea, and it failed to have dramatic impact, especially since the animating equipment was visible.

Richard Fleischer recalls:

> 'We then came up with the idea that this should be done at night, during a storm at sea, so we had spray, waves, and great excitement...so you don't see the flaws. It made it a hundred times more expensive but when we presented the idea to Walt, he said, "You're absolutely right, do it that way".

THE MICKEY MOUSE CLUB

Disney's ability to tackle problems head on, regardless of the costs involved, is based upon his instincts as a gambler. Art Babbitt told film-

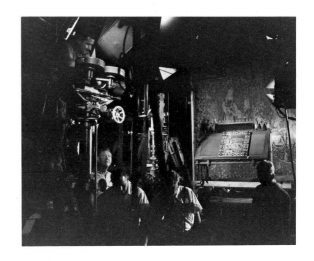

Sleeping Beauty was intended as a lavish spectacular in the tradition of the great pre-war features. The film took six years to make, but it was made at the time when Disney was preoccupied with Disneyland. Expensive production techniques, and absence of Walt's ever-vigilant eye pushed the budget skyward until, as Walt put it, "I had passed the point of no return and I had to go forward with it." Left, top: Animator Marc Davis working on a drawing of Maleficent. Below: Helene Stanley posing for live-action reference. Above: Filming the title shot for the opening sequence.

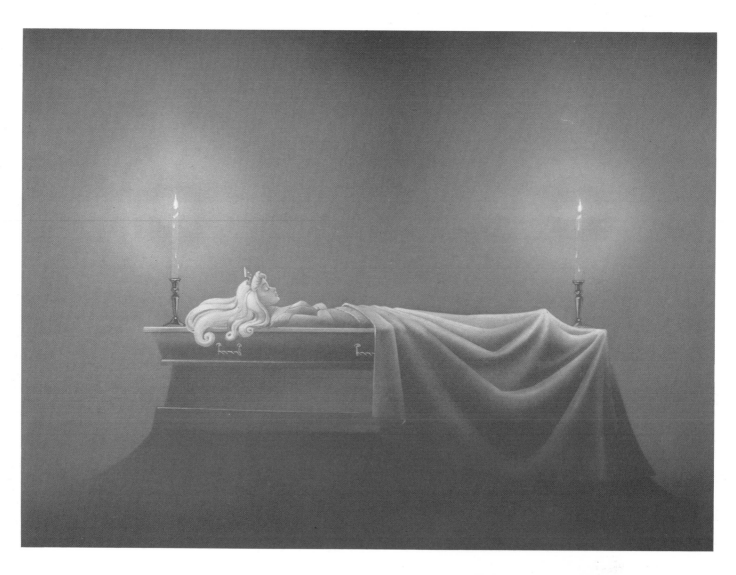

maker-writer John Canemaker that Disney:

> 'was a great gambler, he was willing to take risks for quality, and he surrounded himself with the best talent that was available. He learned very fast, and was a terrific influence...'

In the same year that *20,000 Leagues Under the Sea* was released, Disney launched into television, with Fess Parker in *Davy Crockett, Indian Fighter,* one of the first episodes of the Disneyland series for ABC. Disney's decision to enter television arose from a need to find additional finances for the construction of Disneyland, and the studio created such specialised programs as the regular Mickey Mouse Club, re-establishing Mickey, Donald and Goofy for a new generation of youngsters.

Disneyland was opened on July 17, 1955, at Anaheim, a southern suburb of Los Angeles. A pla-

que there bears the message:

'To all who come to this happy place: Welcome. Disneyland is your land. Here age relives fond memories of the past...and here youth may savour the challenge and promise of the future. Disneyland is dedicated to the ideals, the dreams, and the hard facts that have created America...with the hope that it will be a source of joy and inspiration to all the world.'

As a place designed expressly for entertainment, it has no peers, save the later-built Walt Disney World in Florida. As a realisation of one man's fantasy it is an unparallelled achievement. As a monument to a singularly dedicated genius, Disneyland warrants the inscription found above the north door of St. Paul's Cathedral, London, attributed to the son of Sir Christopher Wren: 'If you would seek his monument, look around.'

Scenes from "Sleeping Beauty" released in 1959. In spite of the dedicated efforts of animators and designers the film failed to impress audiences. Nevertheless it has its moments: Maleficent transforms herself into a fearsome, fire-breathing dragon (above).

Castle Entrance
Fantasy Land

Opposite: *Sleeping Beauty's Castle
as portrayed in the movie.* Above:
*Original sketch for Sleeping Beauty's
Castle at Disneyland, and the castle
being built.*

Although intensely American, Disneyland is also
Swiss in its clinical cleanliness, German in its effi-
ciency, Italian in its breadth of presentation and
theatricality, Japanese in its horticultural harmony,
blessed with a climate that only Californians seem
to enjoy. Its original cost of 17 million dollars has
amply repaid its investors, and it is remarkable that
this dream city, so much part of the Walt Disney
fantasy and flair for showmanship, is now over
twenty-six years old.

It is also remarkable that during this period of
intense creativity, while Disneyland was in the
making, the Disney studio was able to turn out
*Sleeping Beauty, 20,000 Leagues Under the Sea,
Davy Crockett,* and *Lady and The Tramp,* not to

Left: *Sleeping Beauty's Castle at Disneyland, built as a focal-point at the bottom of Main Street.*

213

214

mention forty-six short cartoons, one of which — *Toot, Whistle, Plunk and Boom* – won an Oscar.

MICHELANGELO'S DOG

Lady and the Tramp is classic Disney, one of his most endearing films, and the first animated film to be made in Cinemascope. The story, set like *Peter Pan* at the turn of the century, also opens in the same fashion with a camera panning across the rooftops of a town at night, then trucking in on a lighted window, the new home of 'Lady', the spaniel. Her romance with the mongrel 'Tramp', their combined adventures with dog-catchers, their cosy 'togetherness' scenes when they sit side-by-side on the hill overlooking the town are of necessity delicately handled, since the subject is balanced on the edge of pathos and sentimentality.

The brilliance of the animation, the fine observation of canine behaviour and movement – Tramp shaking off water, or catching a bone thrown for him – and the relationship between cartoon human and cartoon animal – the dogs bark when addressing humans, but speak to each other – admirably meets the challenge. The Italian cooks, Tony and Joe, who serenade the happy pair over spaghetti and meatballs with the song 'Bella Notte' are an outrageous caricature and a sheer delight. There really should be an Italian restaurant like that in every town...

Disneyland is, in effect, Walt's film fantasies brought to reality. Above: Dick Van Dyke on a carousel horse from the film "Mary Poppins".

215

Another successful canine adventure was the live action *Old Yeller*, a boy-and-dog story set on a Texas farm in the 1860s, which reaped a huge profit. Encouraged, the studio dug out an old property 'The Hound of Florence' by Felix Salten, a curious tale

about an apprentice of the Florentine painter Michelangelo, who turned into a dog. Disney decided to modernise the story, and make it into a live-action feature, a comedy about a teenage boy who turns into a shaggy dog – the film's title – casting

"Mary Poppins", adapted from P.L. Traver's book about an English airborne nanny, was one of the most successful movies of all time.

Fred MacMurray and Tommy Kirk. Released in the same year as *Sleeping Beauty*, *The Shaggy Dog* fared much better, and earned almost twice as much as the blockbuster animated feature.

The film did much to give a new lease of life to Fred MacMurray's career – the last major movie starring this versatile actor had been *Double Indemnity*, made fifteen years earlier. *The Shaggy Dog* was followed by *The Absent-Minded Professor*, a quasi science-fiction story that deals with the ever-popular fantasy of flight – the Professor (Fred Mac-Murray) has discovered a substance that defies gravity, allowing some inventive work by the special-effects department, such as having the Professor's car flying over the Disney studios at Burbank.

These films were a further example of the versatility of Disney's attitude to filmmaking – virtually any story and any approach was fair game, although Walt kept a weather eye on the traditional, mainstream subjects. The live-action epic *Swiss Family Robinson*, Johann Wyss's story of the Swiss family of the early 19th century, shipwrecked on a tropical island, and inspired by the adventures of Robinson Crusoe, would seem to have all the ingredients for a Disney success.

A THOUSAND AND ONE SPOTS

Disney put four and a half million dollars into *Swiss Family Robinson*, and for good measure hired British actor John Mills. The atmosphere evoked by *Treasure Island* was not to be repeated, and the film did not live up to expectations. For one thing, *Swiss Family Robinson* lacks the dynamic structure and content of Robert Louis Stevenson's classic; for another, it lacks the dimension and conviction, in spite of the excellent effects.

Darby O'Gill and the Little People (1959) employs special effects with such conviction that the fantasy of 'real' leprechauns almost becomes a reality. In scenes in which the life-size Darby talks and dances with the Lilliputian people, it is impossible to detect the division of the split-screen, or any irregular edges of the matte masking. The effect of the supernatural, with headless coachmen and green horses is admirably conveyed by the use of colour filters, and in some cases shooting the sequence and

Disney's first all live-action feature was "Treasure Island". Left, top: Dennis O'Dea, Bobby Driscoll and Walter Fitzgerald in a port scene. Below: The irreplacable Robert Newton as Long John Silver. Above: Two preliminary story sketches.

running the footage in negative.

In 1961 Walt Disney released his first full-length animated feature with a modern setting, *One Hundred and One Dalmatians*, which also employed a new animation technique, principally devised by Ub Iwerks. This was an adaptation of the Xerox system, a photo-copying process invented by American Chester Carlson as early as 1937, but not perfected until 1950.

Iwerks realised its potential as a means of copying animation drawings on to cels, allowing enormous versatality and a fundamental change of style. The Xerox system produces an electrostatic-

Left: *Long John Silver, Jim Hawkins and pirates from "Treasure Island" released in 1950.*

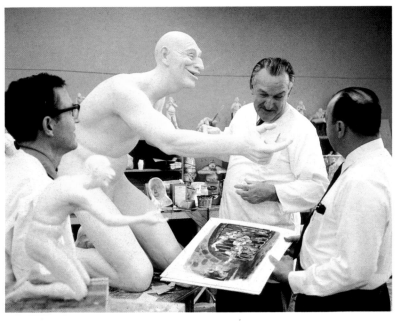

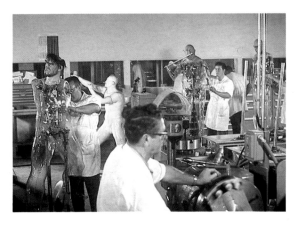

Above and left: *"Pirates of the Caribbean" is one of the most impressive and spectacular adventure rides in Disneyland – a journey by boat through a glittering world of rum-drinking pirates and pirate treasure.*

ally-charged image of pigment particles for transfer on to a specially prepared support. The image, in this case an animal sketch, was transferred by Iwerks' camera on to the cel, thus eliminating the inked lines and capturing all the spontaneity of the original, colour was then applied by hand as usual. The technique led to a looser style of animation, and allowed animators to duplicate drawings, a considerable advantage when you have to animate *One Hundred and One Dalmatians* and their collective one thousand plus spots.

The film is also noteworthy for introducing one of Disney's most fearsome villainesses – the formidable Cruella de Vil, whose principal aim in life is to acquire a Dalamatian-skin coat – 'Cruella de Vil, if she doesn't scare you no evil thing will'… and she sets out to kidnap the puppies who, in one sequence, cover themselves with soot in an attempt at disguise. Like the Queen in *Snow White*, and

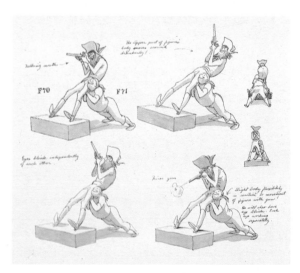

Tableau of pirates and animation study figures. These figures, like President Lincoln and the Hall of Presidents in Walt Disney World, are operated by Audio-Animatronics (see following caption).

Maleficent in *Sleeping Beauty*, this latest in a fine tradition of wicked ladies is accorded a certain degree of fashionable elegance, the more to emphasise her duplicity and evil intent, since she is a grotesque caricature of one of Avedon's angular couture models of the early 1960s.

SWAN SONG

Disney went back to medieval England for his next animated feature, an Arthurian romance adapted from T. H. White's book 'The Sword in the Stone', with its stirring message 'Whoso pulleth out this sword of this stone and anvil, is rightwise king born of all England.' The story is, in many respects, ideal Disney material. Arthur, or 'Wart' is suitably skinny and tow-headed, and the film dwells on his education by the magician Merlin, who is accompanied by his 'familiar', an owl known as Archimedes. Yensid, the sorcerer from *Fantasia*, would have made a much better Merlin, and there's a sequence in which unaided brooms sweep the floor, bringing us faint echoes of 'The Sorcerer's Apprentice'.

The Sword in the Stone failed on all levels except the animation, and anybody who feared that Disney might be losing his touch was soon to be proven wrong by the excellence of *The Jungle Book*, and the Supercalifragilisticexpialidocious *Mary Poppins*, one of the most successful movies ever made.

Mary Poppins was Walt Disney's magnum opus,

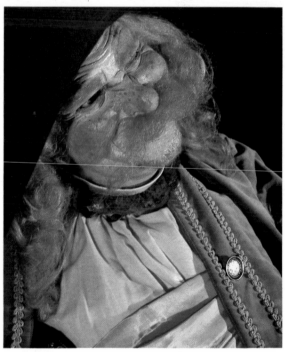

his grand finale, and also his swan song. The film was released in 1964 and Disney died in 1966 of lung cancer, in the hospital opposite the Studio on South Buena Vista Street. It should be mentioned that Disney had been a heavy smoker for most of his life, the cigarettes aggravating a regular cough that became a famous characteristic, especially in the studio where it heralded his immediate appearance.

Mary Poppins' outstanding success owes much to its vitality, its exuberance and its sureness. Disney knew exactly what he was doing, and exactly how P. L. Travers's book should be adapted. It is, more than anything else, a showman's film and Disney, as we know, was a showman par excellence.

The story is about an English nanny in London in the early 1900s. Not, one might think, the ideal subject for a Disney film – but this nanny is different, she can *fly*, a magic ingredient that made the book very appealing to Disney's sense of fantasy. He approached Mrs. Travers, who was less than enthusiastic, and not overly impressed by this offer from a Hollywood tycoon to purchase the rights to her book. She declined, and Disney spent several frustrating years persuading her to change her mind in his favour.

Disney, essentially the cartoonmaker, had first visualised the story as an animated feature, and it is understandable that the author lacked the same vision and treatment of her creation. Mary Poppins,

The voices and movements of Audio-Animatronics figures can be awesomely lifelike. The articulated muscles and joints, even the eye and lip movements, are controlled from within the figure by electronic impulses, prerecorded on a multi-track tape.

albeit airborne, was decidedly not a Disney cartoon. Walt then suggested a combination of live-action and animation — it didn't much matter either way since he was well equipped to handle both mediums, the main thing was that Walt Disney's conception was infinitely entertaining. It was an interesting clash of wills: Walt could be charmingly persuasive, but Mrs. Travers was an Australian with a no-nonsense attitude to life. The Disney charm prevailed, and the project was finally given the go-ahead.

A SPOONFUL OF SUGAR

Disney decided that his main character, Mary Poppins, should be younger and more engaging than Mrs. Travers's middle-aged, starched nanny. He had considered both Mary Martin and Bette Davis for the role, but eventually plumped for the star of the stage version of *My Fair Lady*, Julie Andrews because, according to various reports, 'he liked the way she whistled'. Dick Van Dyke was cast as Bert,

The Blue Bayou Lagoon – in the centre of which stands a thriving restaurant – from the "Pirates of the Caribbean", at Disneyland. Above: During construction of the Jungle Cruise, Disneyland.

227

on the strength of the currently popular Dick Van Dyke Show, while Robert and Richard Sherman were commissioned to write the songs, most of which became hits: 'A Spoonful of Sugar', 'Chim-Chim-Cheree', and 'Feed the Birds'.

According to Bob Thomas in his Walt Disney biography, 'Feed the Birds' made Walt cry every time he heard it. 'That song'll replace Brahms' Lullaby,' Walt declared. *Mary Poppins* was directed by Robert Stevenson, with visual effects by Peter Ellenshaw, who had worked on *20,000 Leagues*.

The combination of live-action and animation is well suited to the plot of 'Mary Poppins' in which the nanny works magic to conduct the children through a (cartoon) fantasy world.

The film's vitality and confidence overcomes the flaws, such as Dick Van Dyke's Cockney accent which sometimes sounds as though his mouth were

Water plays an important part of the various adventure rides in Disneyland, transporting the passengers through such locations as the "Jungle Cruise". Top picture: Walt Disney supervises the installation of animals during construction.

228

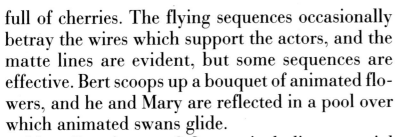

full of cherries. The flying sequences occasionally betray the wires which support the actors, and the matte lines are evident, but some sequences are effective. Bert scoops up a bouquet of animated flowers, and he and Mary are reflected in a pool over which animated swans glide.

Mary Poppins won 5 Oscars, including a special effects Oscar, and Julie Andrews was named 'Best Actress of the Year'.

The Jungle Book, released in 1967, virtually marks the end of Walt Disney's career, although *The Happiest Millionaire* came out at the same time. *The Jungle Book* moreover, is a cartoon feature, and one of the most popular ever made by the studio, and Disney was, in essence, the most

successful cartoon-maker of all time. It is a film
full of delicate touches and finely observed traits,
such as Bagheera the panther, lounging on the
branch of a tree, the tip of his tail lazily curling
and uncurling. Loosely based on Rudyard Kipling's original, *The Jungle Book* tells the story
of an orphan, abandoned in the jungle, but saved
by the efforts of Bagheera, who leaves him to
be raised by a family of wolves. When the infant reaches boyhood, the animals decide that he
must be returned to mankind, especially since his
life is threatened by the arrival of Shere Khan, the
tiger.

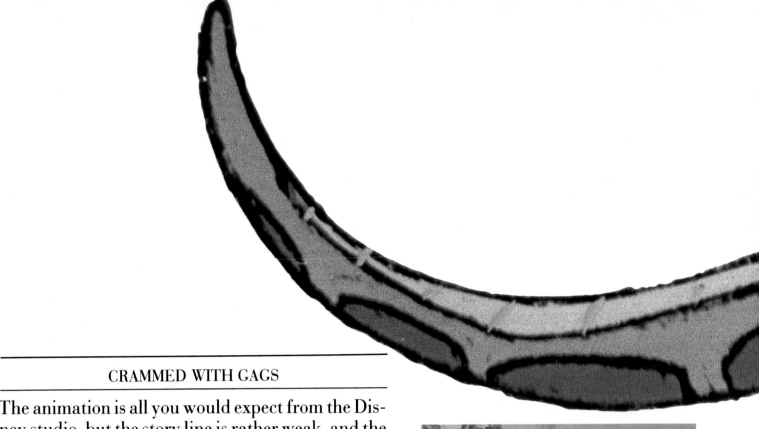

CRAMMED WITH GAGS

The animation is all you would expect from the Disney studio, but the story line is rather weak, and the film leans heavily on voice characterization. This treatment, used by other studios, was relatively new for Disney, and a reversal of traditional procedures. Actors begin by building up the character from the script, to which animators supply the visual. Sometimes it is difficult to associate the suave and silky voice of George Sanders with the animated tiger, or the voice of Phil Harris with Baloo the Bear. Sterling Holloway's sibilant hypnotising Kaa the cobra is wonderful, a creature that animals learn to avoid, and Colonel Hathi, leader of the Elephants' Patrol, has faint echoes of Dumbo, but the musical treatment by the Sherman brothers strikes an odd note, especially when the boy Mowgli breaks into a song-and-dance routine in the jungle.

Nevertheless, *The Jungle Book* is a thoroughly enjoyable and entertaining film, directed by Wolfgang Reitherman, with some fine background paintings. The film influenced, in many ways, the animated feature *Robin Hood*, also directed by Reitherman, using the voices of character actors to support the cartoon figures.

Robin Hood was released in 1973, and is one of the funniest films ever produced by the Disney Studio, partly due to the performance of Peter Ustinov, Terry-Thomas and Phil Harris, and to animators

"The Jungle Book", adapted from the story by Rudyard Kipling, was one of Disney's most enjoyable cartoon features – it was also his last, being released the year following his death in 1966. Left: Background scenes from the film. Above: The boy Mowgli with his friend Baloo the Bear, whose voice was that of the comedian Phil Harris.

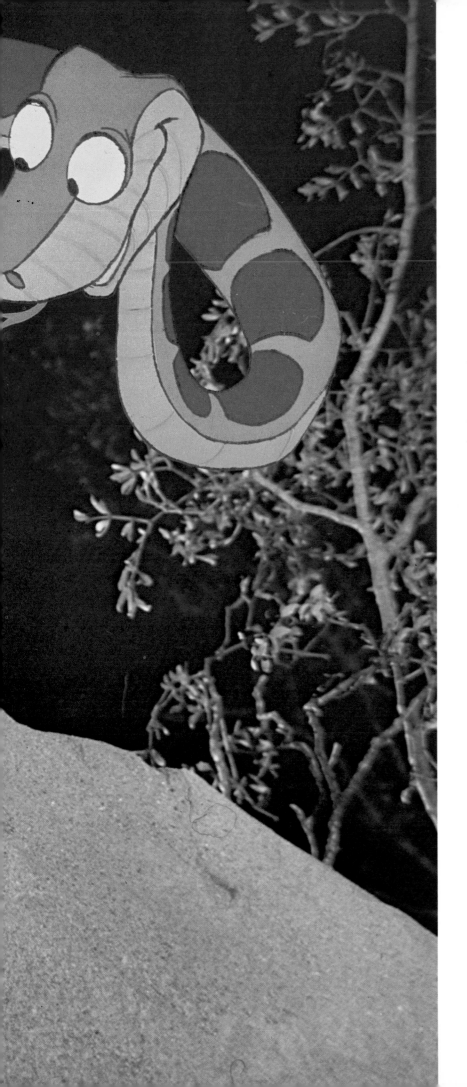

Gerbil from the nature classic "The Living Desert" with the snake Kaa – an expert at hypnosis – from "The Jungle Book".

Frank Thomas, Milt Kahl and Ollie Johnston, and Ken Anderson's production.

Ustinov plays Prince John, a petulant lion with psychological problems and a deep sense of insecurity—he sucks his thumb and calls for his mother. He aims blows at his adviser, a snake called Sir Hiss, 'Hiss! You deliberately dodged', who shares with *The Jungle Book's* Kaa an ability to hypnotise. 'Hypnosis' says Hiss sibilantly, 'will rid you of your psychosis.'

The animators drew finely on caricature to portray the snake with a gap between his teeth, a feature of actor Terry-Thomas, who provides the snake's voice, 'A mere slip of the forked tongue, your majesty.' The film is crammed with the gags that became the Disney trademark, and ends like a Keystone Cops comedy, with a troop of Hippos trapped in a tent, which blindly demolishes every-

thing in its path.

A memorable gag has Sir Hiss imprisoned in an ale barrel by being forced into the bung-hole and the bung replaced. 'But I don't drink,' comes the muffled protest. Disney would have been delighted and reassured by the success of these post-Disney cartoons, and in one sense the master's touch reached out from the past, because some of the animation drawings were based on originals for *Snow White*.

It is not unusual for animators to re-use sequences from previous cartoons, or to use the same action several times. Xerox cels helped to swell the ranks of the 101 Dalmations, and the 'morgue' in the Burbank studios is a valuable source of animation reference for new animators.

A POT-BELLIED DRAGON

In 1973, it was decided to employ and train a new group of animators, specifically to maintain the traditions and the quality that Disney fought so hard to establish. The aim was further extended to replace the famous team of founder-animators, dubbed by Walt the 'Nine Old Men' – Les Clark, Frank Thomas, Ward Kimball, Ollie Johnston, Marc Davis, Milt Kahl, John Lounsbery, Eric Larson and Woolie Reitherman. Ken Anderson, designer and one-time story man, famous for having once set fire to Disney's moustache, said that 'the

The success of "Seal Island" in 1949 inspired several similar projects, such as "The African Lion" (above) also filmed by Al and Elma Milotte. Also pictured, "The Living Desert" (left and top above).

new team...have the same kind of drive and ambition we had in the '30s. Nothing is beyond them.'

The team were responsible for work on *The Rescuers*, directed by Reitherman, which critic Leonard Maltin declares:

> 'is the best cartoon feature to come from the studio since *101 Dalmatians* more than fifteen years before. It has what so many other animated films have lacked—heart.'

Pete's Dragon followed in 1977, a live-action/animation feature that starred a mild-mannered, pot-bellied dragon called Elliott, designed by Anderson, with a cast comprising Mickey Rooney, Shelley Winters, Helen Reddy, and Elliott's friend Pete, played by twelve-year-old Sean Marshall.

Even without Walt the production costs mounted, as the legacy of perfection was observed. A stretch of the Maine coastline, and a nineteenth century Maine village was reconstructed on Morro Bay, California, at a cost of 250,000 dollars. A further 115,000 was needed to build a lighthouse, complete with a specially made period lens, which could cast a beam up to twenty-five miles. A Disney lighthouse doesn't merely have to look authentic, it has to *work*.

THE 'IMAGINEER'

Looking back on the astonishing career of this ex railroad candy butcher, ambulance driver, news-

paper boy, advertising designer, cartoonist and film producer, what can be said in conclusion? For one thing, Disney himself never looked back, but always looked very hard at the present and very far into the future. The last film that Disney made, and one in which he starred, was not for general public release, but for the people of Florida and the Press, and its purpose was to describe Walt's dream of the future. The dream embraced a messianic vision of a city twice the size of Manhattan, to be constructed at an estimated cost of a billion dollars. The city would be established in Florida, financed by free enterprise, and it would be called – or rather, the project would be called – EPCOT, the 'Experimental Prototype Community of Tomorrow'. The project began near Orlando, Florida and fulfilled the first requirement in that the site was twice the size of Manhattan.

"The Incredible Journey" directed by Fletcher Markle, was basically a nature film built around a truelife story about three domestic pets who crossed a continent. Above: *101 Dalmatians minus ninety-eight.*

.....and the remainder of the cast. "101 Dalmatians" owes its free, style to Ub Iwerks' adaption of the Xerox camera which allowed animators to short-cut traditional techniques, and thus preserve the spontaneity of animation sketches.

A37

Above and overleaf: *the appalling Cruella de Vil, one of the best of the Disney villainesses, and a modern version of Medusa. Overleaf, right: The Haunted Mansion in Florida's Walt Disney World, built in the style of an English Manor house.*

On this site Disney's 'imagineers' constructed a sequel to Disneyland, the now famous Walt Disney World containing that remarkable urban complex, the Magic Kingdom, with its conservation park and fleet of submarines — said to be the fifth largest in the world, and the Lake Buena Vista community, a New Town that just begins to approach Disney's EPCOT ideals, planned to house 16,500 residents and 4,000 workers.

The Magic Kingdom is a living museum and entertainment centre, comprising Adventureland, Fantasyland, Frontierland, Main Street, Liberty

Square, and Tomorrowland, described by architect Peter Blake as 'a marvellous and absolutely stupefying piece of giant confectionery, a kind of Candy Kremlin...'

Disney's vision of the future never dwelt on the pessimism of George Orwell's '1984', but on the optimism of H. G. Wells' 'Things to Come', a true democracy and a pragmatical community which supported the progress of family life. He had invited his audience to believe that fairy tales could come true. Now he merely wanted them to put such beliefs to practice.

THE SELF-MADE FANTASY

It has often been claimed that no one really knew Walt Disney, that the 'real' Walt hid behind a

Hollywood producers and designers have had a lot of experience in recreating European haunted sites: Dracula's Castle and Frankenstein's Castle were archetypal settings. Modern techniques and Disney Audio-Animatronics have contributed some unnerving and realistic touches that is, if you believe in ghosts...Overleaf: Walt Disney World at nightfall.

facade, that he held a key that might unlock some vital element of his persona. There is supposed to be a lot of Walt in the character of Mickey Mouse, the carefree, fun-loving, sociable figure dedicated to the entertainment of his audience, the audience to which Disney continually referred during story conferences, and when planning a script. 'Pleasing the public', he once wrote, 'is one of the most difficult tasks in the world.'

Therein lies a possible clue to Walt Disney's drive and ambition. There is a further clue in the photograph of Walt, standing in a proprietorial attitude beneath a window in Disneyland's Main Street. On the window are lettered the words, 'Elias Disney. Contractor. Est. 1895'. The man who built, with his

own hands, the Chicago house in which Walt was born, the man to whom Walt was probably closer than anyone in his childhood years, and the one who was always so difficult to please.

Elias Disney contributed a great deal to Walt's singleminded search for fulfilment. Elias was the audience whose approval Walt eagerly sought, the father which Disney himself in so many ways resembled. He ruled over his world of fantasy with a magic wand, and that world will forever bear the stamp of his genius, and his name:

WALT DISNEY.

Disneyland was a natural development of the Disney dream, which began in two dimensions and finally became three — some would say four. Its message is simple, its aims a judicious blend of altruism and commercialism.

INDEX

ACKNOWLEDGEMENTS

WE WOULD LIKE TO THANK everyone within
the Walt Disney organization who has helped us in
the production of this book, particularly Keith
Bales, Vince Jefferds, Don MacLaughlin, Wendall
Mohler, Wayne Morris, Pat Lawson, David Smith
and staff, LeRoy Anderson and staff, and of course
all those people who have made things possible
within the studio at Burbank.